"As a teenager, Karina Robertson was an outlier. Her faith ran deep. Her love for family was clear. And her desire to serve Christ with abandon was constant. Karina was gentle and still passionate, living large yet as focused as any adult, and crazy fun yet still deeply insightful. But the most remarkable gift Karina gave to us was the ability to make anyone feel like she was her best friend. *Anchored* gives us the chance to get a glimpse of this amazing young woman's heart, faith, and life."

> Chap Clark, PhD
> Author, *Hurt 2.0: Inside the world of today's teenagers*
> Professor of Youth, Family, and Culture
> Fuller Theological Seminary

"Out of unspeakable pain that can only be known by a mother who has lost a daughter, Katie Robertson reveals a story so grounded in the steadfast strength of God's love that it had to be titled *Anchored*. Her story illuminates a pathway of hope and healing for all of us.

> Dr. Leslie Parrott
> Author, *You Matter More Than You Think*
> Seattle Pacific University

"This book is packed with road tested and real life wisdom. What a privilege to be invited on Karina's journey of faith and family."

> Rick Enloe
> Pastor, Harbor Christian Center
> Gig Harbor, Washington

"Hope is a mysterious thing. We know that it is real, but we don't know what it really is. We know that God created it, that it is we who must discover it. Katie takes us along with her on the universal path of discovery, hand in hand with the Lord, through a menagerie of understandable hopes. Then she shows us how a God-given *ability to hope* sustained them all through Karina's illness, but ultimately it is only One Hope which sustains them today. God created us with an imagination that we might better understand the hints of truth and glory He has placed in our lives. Katie shows us how to use it, not to create imaginary things, but to better understand the real things of God, and to fortify a hope that can fuel our lives."

Rob Lane, MD, retired oncologist

ANCHORED

Walking by Faith, Living in Hope,
Remembering Karina

Katie Robertson and Caroline Timmins

Library of Congress Cataloging-in-Publication Data

Robertson, Katie and Timmins, Caroline.
        Anchored: walking by faith, living in hope, remembering Karina/ Katie Robertson and Caroline Timmins.

ISBN-13:
978-0615793320 (Katie\Robertson)

ISBN-10:
0615793320

Questions, comments, or speaking engagements, contact Katie

Robertson at: katiejr@comcast.net

"We have this **HOPE**

[Jesus]

as an anchor for the soul,

FIRM AND SECURE."

Hebrews 6:19

Katie and Karina Robertson, mother and daughter

About the authors...

Katie Robertson*: "For a long time, I wanted to share with others the unfailing love God showed our family in the years we faced cancer with Karina. The words were in my heart, but I knew I could not do it alone. I prayed for the Lord to help me, confident He would use our experience to encourage others. Karina's walk of faith was truly amazing and I wanted people to glimpse the hope which anchored her, and us, along our journey.*

Meeting Caroline was such an awesome answer to this prayer. It felt like the Lord brought us together to accomplish what was to me, an overwhelming task: the writing of this book. Its completion shows me yet again, how God can take our deepest dreams and turn them into reality. It is truly a testament to His faithful provision in my life.

Karina's life was short but so full and lived in faith. The way she handled the storms that came along, remaining anchored on the Lord, serves as an example for all of us. From the time Karina entered our world, we imparted our faith to her. And as she made her exit, her enduring trust in Him touched us deeply. What we passed on to her, returned to bless us. Karina Jean was not only my daughter and friend, but also my inspiration in following Jesus, and depending on Him, for everything. She will not be forgotten. Instead, her legacy will carry on for generations through the many people whose lives she touched. It is my sincere hope and prayer that you find this book not only an interesting read, but thought-provoking as well. May it help you to grow your roots deep in your relationship with God that you, too, may experience His unfailing love."

Katie graduated from the University of Washington, and is a teacher, an artist, a runner, and a full-time mom to Erik, a high school junior, and Annika, a sophomore at the University of Washington. She and her husband, Ron, live in Gig Harbor, Washington, where they continue to enjoy their seaside home and many boating adventures. The family remains actively involved with fund-raising efforts for Malibu, Young Life, and the Fred Hutchinson Cancer Research Center of Seattle, for which some of the proceeds from this book will be apportioned.

Caroline Timmins, LMFT: *"Meeting Katie has been a blessing and privilege. While she was praying for a writer, I was praying for a story. Since I first learned to weave words together in second grade, I have loved the craft of writing. I have often wondered if that passion would ever serve a greater purpose. Thus, using my skills to develop a poignant memoir of the Robertson's faith and hope has been especially meaningful. As a counselor, I am trained to listen to the stories of others and to ask questions aimed at uncovering previously unrecognized thoughts or feelings. But to actually immerse myself into the life of another and attempt to write in such a way that those thoughts and feelings form a coherent text, has required an interesting blend of creativity and therapeutic ability. Working with Katie and observing her deep faith, her optimism and joy, and her artistic approach to life, has inspired me greatly.*

Someone has said, 'We read to know we're not alone.' Pain can be such a lonely place. I trust this book will help others who are experiencing a faith crisis, or dealing with the loss of a child, to find renewed hope, and be reassured they are not alone in their suffering for, 'God…is not far from each one of us' Romans 17: 27-28."

Caroline has an undergraduate degree from Biola University, and a Master's in Marriage and Family Therapy from Seattle Pacific University. In addition to being a licensed marriage and family therapist, she is a writer, artist, and mom to two active teenagers. Caroline and her family are natives of the Pacific Northwest, but relocated to Buffalo, New York, in 2012. She is in the process of developing a counseling practice in the suburb of Williamsville.

Karina Jean Robertson

Contents

Forward by Brandon Heath   9
Introduction: Anchored in Faith   11

1. Gone From My Sight   15
2. Young Life and Malibu   27
3. Inlet Love   30
4. Our Love of Boating   36
5. Anchored at Home   42
6. Epiphany   57
7. Anchoring Kids in Faith   68
8. Karina's Anchored Faith   74
9. Anchored in the Storm   89
10. Anchored Amid Fear   102
11. One Mind, One Marrow   108
12. Three Perfect Years   132
13. Final Diagnosis   159
14. Facing the Enemy   168
15. Anchored until the End   176
16. Rocks and Rainbows   182
17. Anchored and Rooted   198

Epilogue   208
Afterward   214
For Karina by Rob Lane, MD oncology   222
Tips for anchoring your children in faith   229
Anchor Points of Faith   231
Simple gifts for helping those who grieve   232
Acknowledgements   235
End Notes   237

Forward
Brandon Heath

Grammy-nominated Contemporary Christian Music Singer / Songwriter
March 2013

I remember writing my first song. I had just gotten my first guitar only the day before and already the words were flowing. It was therapy. It was soul searching. It was amazing. I feel strongly that we all have in ourselves, the God-given ability to heal others, ironically, even with our own pain. I sense that is Katie Robertson's goal with *Anchored*, a deeply personal memoir of some of the happiest and most painful days of her life.

I met the Robertson family when I was in my early 20's. We share a deep love for a place called Malibu, a Young Life camp in British Columbia, Canada. There is a long, rich history of faith and family there. Though most of us are not related at all, we are very much family. When one of us hurts, we all hurt. It is this community that I have leaned on in some of the most difficult times in my life. Malibu is also where I began my relationship with Jesus as a 15 year old. The Young Life kids who came there in the late 90's and early 2000's were the first people to hear my music. It was this sense of family that gave me the courage to share, not only my weaknesses, but my desires and dreams, with people far beyond that secluded inlet in the Canadian Cascades.

Malibu was particularly special to their daughter, Karina, whom I had the privilege of meeting at our favorite spot on earth. She lost her life to cancer, fought an amazingly hard battle with leukemia, and left behind her a legacy of love and faith in Christ. The Robertson's are a very inclusive and magnetic bunch. Karina was an integral part of that chemistry. Her loss will be felt for a long time, but there was a great lesson of love that stayed with us.

I so admire Katie's bravery to open up about those difficult months, but also the moments of great peace and trust in the Lord. She has anchored herself to the truth. There is confidence in knowing that you are tied to a loving God, who is unchangeable amid the ebbs and flows of this world.

Nashville, Tennessee

9

Introduction: Anchored in Faith
Caroline Timmins, LMFT

The Pacific Northwest was in the midst of a brilliant autumn season the week I flew out to work on our book. I sat on the Robertson's deck mesmerized by the generous October sun as it sparkled like a million diamonds on the water before me. Mt. Rainier loomed hazy but majestic on the horizon while seagulls screeched their chorus overhead. There is an unmatched beauty to this place.

Yet amid the rich bounty of this lovely home there exists a deep void. It is the sadness of losing a child. Life still vibrates within the walls. Visitors frequent. Meals are shared. Wine is poured. Prayers are, amazingly, still offered. Some people may have given up on God by now: their impassioned pleas for the life of their child seemingly ignored. Indeed it is easy to question the love of a God who seems to turn His back on those who have spent their earthly lives in His service. God does seem to run reckless with people at times. I stare out over the peaceful shore and ponder how He can be at the same time, as consistently faithful as the tide, yet as wildly unpredictable as a brewing storm.

One thing amazing to me is the resilience of the human spirit. That a person can survive tragedy or atrocity, injury or injustice or just plain old-fashioned gut wrenching loss; the kind that knocks one down on their face in the mud heaving in tears; and eventually get up again to resume the business of living is to me, nothing short of a miracle. But combine that with getting up still loyal to the one supposedly in control of it all. How many of us weather hardship with our faith in a loving God still intact? A tenacious faith that says, perhaps through tired tears or even angry sobs: "Though He slay me (or my daughter) yet I will trust Him" (Job 13:15).

Yet, this is the kind of faith that dwells here, in this seaside home. It may be a tarnished faith, thread bare and bewildered, but nevertheless it is still faith. The salt from the sea can corrode the surface of a boat's anchor, yet it still holds firm in a storm. No one said faith had to be pretty, only substantial.

It is this type of anchored faith I first witnessed when I met Katie nearly two years ago. At that time I remember feeling a strange sense of privilege which may sound odd since she had come to me for grief counseling.

Karina had died earlier that year. Still, as I sat in that sacred place of shared sorrow I glimpsed her resolute spirit. Katie had endured heart wrenching sadness yet remained determined to embrace the deeper story.

She was not ignorant of her less productive ways of dealing with grief. Katie is a doer. While some may stay in bed, over eat or drink, or turn a blind eye as their spaces accumulate the debris of depression, Katie runs. Running helps. It gives her strength. She keeps moving. She stays busy, sometimes to her detriment. Dealing well with loss involves facing it straight on. There is no escaping its bitter darkness. The only way out is through. That is the deep soul work that must accompany grief. Yet, amid or perhaps during that recovery, she refused to park permanently in introspection. As she spoke from the shattered soul of a mother, she shared her dream of writing "the Karina story." She felt there was a deeper script worth sharing and she wanted to get it on paper before she forgot the details.

Thus began the exercise of her telling me those bits and pieces of Karina's life she was remembering each week and me recording them. As she shared the deep faith of her daughter, and the mini miracles that had occurred along the way, I began to share in her excitement of a book. The faith she and her daughter lived was not a stale set of religious rules. Instead, it was living and breathing and, well, muscled. As a therapist, I knew it was the kind of brilliant faith hurting families need in the midst of dark days. I listened to Katie's story and had no doubt it was one other people would find inspiring. But in the crisis times of life, when the losses are overwhelming, faith needs to be more than inspiring. It needs to be sturdy enough to carry a young person to her grave, and durable enough to securely hold those who are left behind to navigate the void. It needs to hold firm like an anchor. People are looking for that kind of faith, and when they find it, they desperately want to know how to pass it on to their children. Katie has that kind of faith, and through years of living, breathing, talking and praying she passed it on to her daughter along with a most precious gift: the assurance of eternal life through Jesus Christ.

Our therapeutic work together ended when I injured my back and needed a medical leave. She found another counselor to facilitate her healing. I found a surgeon to facilitate mine. Time passed, but eventually, we reconnected. By now, our relationship had changed to one of story teller/writer and we set about the serious task of crafting a book. To honor

Karina's love of scrapbooking, we also created photo collages using papers from her own collection, entries from her prayer journals, and sketches by Katie and Annika. As we fell into a compatible partnership, I continued to see glimpses of Katie's tenacious faith and hope.

She reminded me of the words from the Old Testament book of Jeremiah 17:7-8 (gender changed for effect):

"Blessed is the woman who trusts in the Lord, whose confidence is in Him, she is like a tree planted by the water, she has no worries in time of drought and never fails to bear fruit."

If ever our souls are in a time of drought, it is in the aftermath of great loss. And of the many losses in life, the death of a child is one most severe. Our children are our hope and our future. In them we live on even as we age, knowing they will carry our legacy. They are the seeds we plant, water, feed and nurture. Like a prized rosebush, we long to see them bloom and flourish. Thus, when they are taken from us, it feels as if the air has drained from our own lungs. The sorrow can be suffocating.

Katie still grieves deeply. There are times when a photo, a song or a memory ignites tears. More and more, however, they are tears of gratefulness for years given rather than bitterness over years lost. Time does not heal the raw wound, but it does help to incorporate the void into reality. In short, time helps a person get used to loss, but the emptiness will linger like an unwelcome shadow. Even so, there is a quality to Katie's pain that is fruitful. She has chosen to plant even in this season of drought. This book is that seed.

In telling the story of Karina, she is reliving some painful memories in hopes of giving the reader a sense of the wonderful life Karina lived and the rich road of faith she traveled from a very small child, through her junior high and high school years, as a cancer patient, as a person overcoming cancer, as a young person achieving the dream of college, and as a woman dying from the resurgence of this awful disease. Through all of these winding curves in her life, Karina held tightly to a faith in the one who is able to save, Jesus Christ. It is really His story, the story of how He invades our human existence and offers hope in the face of our deepest fear - the fear of death.

I was not privileged to meet Karina in this life. Through the stories of a parent who loved her dearly, I have glimpsed this incredible young woman. I fully believe she would be happy to know her mom is turning a season of drought into a season of harvest. I also think Karina would want readers to grasp the deep mystery of the good news of Jesus Christ which in this world must be taken on faith, but in her world, is more real than we could ever imagine.

One of Karina's favorite authors penned it best in the last paragraph of his final book in the Narnia series (gender changed for effect):

"All (her) life in this world and all (her) adventures....had only been the cover and the title page: now at last (she) was beginning Chapter One of the Great Story which no one on earth has read: which goes on forever: in which every chapter is better than the one before."

The Last Battle by C. S. Lewis.

Buffalo, New York
November 2012

Chapter 1: Gone From my Sight--That is all

Our boat, *Epiphany*, skims the inky blue depths of the Puget Sound en route to favorite havens. Although we are one less crew member now, the places we love hold reminders of her. At Roche Harbor in the San Juan Islands of Washington State, a tree grows above her ashes, and at Young Life's Malibu Club in British Columbia, a pair of benches honor her memory. From their perch above the rapids they beckon campers to a moment of quiet contemplation amid the frenzied activity of summer camp. Our girl would have liked that. She was a contemplative soul.

Boating on the inlets of the Puget Sound and British Columbia has always been a rejuvenating experience for our family. We return every summer for excursions in and around our favorite shores. In years past, our girls, Karina and Annika, would bring along their dolls as seaworthy guests, and spend hours giggling together as best friends, their heads bent over in play. On sunny afternoons, Erik would commandeer the dinghy to small, protected islands, claiming them for his own with a stick planted decisively like an explorer's flag. As a family, we created many happy memories together, wading in the sun-warmed shallows or lying on deck beneath a full moon. The natural rock pools carved by centuries of crashing waves, brought hours of shared discovery and squeals of delight as the kids found colorful sea life hiding within. In the peaceful, majestic beauty of these rugged cliffs, surrounded by my happy, healthy family, it was easy to feel a sense of heaven on earth. Nature is just one of the many gifts we have received from our generous Creator.

Children are another amazing gift from God and I was blessed with three. Karina Jean, my precious first-born daughter, was my special treasure from the day she was born. We had such an easy connection and she had grown into a cherished friend. She was also the best sister in the world to Annika and Erik, as well as a real daddy's girl, with her unquenchable desire for new information. Like my husband, Ron, she loved a lively conversation around a good topic.

Every day, in so many ways, I am reminded of her. The permanency of her death penetrates my thoughts often but is never fully absorbed. And, although the once ferocious sting has become less piercing with time, her actual death still remains an intensely painful memory.

When we dropped her off for her freshman year at Seattle Pacific University, there were tearful goodbyes, and a definite void was felt around our house. We adjusted to being a family of four during the week, but living so close to the school had its benefits. I was able to meet her, along with the new friends she was making, for lunch on campus every Tuesday, and she often returned to our home in Gig Harbor for weekend visits. Now, however, her place at the dinner table has become permanently vacant.

I believe wholeheartedly I will see Karina again one day. This is the most comforting hope of my Christian faith: the promise of eternal life after death - a life free from sadness, sickness, pain, and loss. Hebrews 6:19 says: "We have this hope [Jesus] as the anchor for the soul, firm and secure." There is nothing else in this world that offers me an assured forever promise like that. I am at the same time full of great hope and great sadness. I miss her so much. I know I must do my best to press on, continue to love well and keep the faith, but, for now, I can only await that future day. Living in the "not yet" is a long, lonely stretch. Death still stings.

During the last three weeks of Karina's life, a little voice kept creeping into my mind. It was gentle but persistent, not to be ignored. "Katie," it queried, "even if I do not answer your prayers in the way you want, will you still trust me? Will you still honor me?"

I knew it was the voice of God, for that is how He often speaks, in a persistent whisper slighter than a thought. It was the same voice I first heard years ago, when I was only twelve. I was at a concert listening to Seattle pastor Wayne Taylor talk about God. Sitting in the front row apart from my identical twin, who was seated behind me for some reason, was a rare occurrence. We were usually inseparable. What she did, I did. I followed her lead. But in this most sacred moment I was alone, just me, with my thoughts focused entirely on the speaker.

Wayne described how we can enter a personal relationship with Jesus Christ. He explained Him as *the* way, *the* truth and *the* life" (John 14:6). I had never thought about accepting Jesus Christ and having Him as my friend, and the prospect thrilled me. At that moment the voice said, "Katie, I love you, follow me." The Lord Jesus was inviting me into a real and living relationship. Why hadn't someone told me this sooner? I could hardly contain my excitement. In that moment, sitting by myself, not concerned about anyone or anything else, I stood up and chose to give my whole heart to follow Him for the rest of my days. I realize it sounds fictional. But for those who have accepted and experienced His love, it is powerful and transforming. In that moment, I said yes.

That day marked the beginning of my friendship with Jesus. But what my twelve year old self could not yet understand was the depth of the gift I had received. The Lord's personal invitation to my young responsive heart would shape not only the course of my life, but also that of my daughter's. In a legacy of enduring faith, I would pass on to her my belief in Christ, and that faith would solidify into the unshakeable foundation which anchored Karina till the very end.

The friendship begun that day has influenced every part of my life: my career choice, my marriage, my volunteer time, and my parenting. I have come to know God as a real person, someone who is interested in all that concerns me. I have never doubted His love; He convinced me of it that first night. However, I have been plenty confused, at times, by why things happen the way they do. Many times things have not made sense, and Karina's death was one of them. You would think a God of love would never allow difficult, painful things to happen to his friends. But, He sometimes does. I do not fully know why. There are certain questions I have stopped asking. He is, after all, the same God who created the universe. Surely He is bigger, wiser and far more intelligent than me. At times like this, I am reminded He is God, and I have two choices: submit and trust, or fight and demand a different answer. I choose the first.

Still, as I sat at Karina's side watching her lose this long battle with cancer, it was through tears and a shattered heart that I answered, "Yes, Lord, I **will** still trust you and honor you. I **will** give you glory no matter what."

I knew from the beginning of Karina's battle that my attitude would be one of trust. I held firmly to the promise of Psalms 9:10:

"Those who know your name will trust in you, for you Lord, have never forsaken those who seek you."

I knew I would trust God fully, whatever the outcome, for I had come to believe His love for me. He had proven himself faithful even when the way was uncertain and circumstances did not make sense. It is definitely difficult to trust when there is a lack of clarity. But when faced with the baffling dilemma of pain, suffering, and loss, we are called to walk by faith, not by sight, and to trust even when things do not make sense. Many times He had answered with the words and actions for which I hoped. Twice he healed Karina. Twice He gave her more time with us. In the end, however, she died. I do not understand why; nevertheless, I choose to trust Him.

The loss of Karina is still devastating to our family. Even now, three years later, my husband and I have many days of questioning and wondering why God would take our daughter from us so early in her life. She was such a bright light in our lives and in the lives of so many in our community and beyond. She had a remarkable presence. It is hard for us to fathom her death on April 26, 2010.

At the same time of year when, in history, Jesus Christ was falsely accused, beaten, and hung on a cross, our daughter endured the worst kind of pain. Like Jesus, she never complained. I shriveled in the corner of the ICU watching my daughter's illness steal away her vitality and life. How can words portray the agony of watching one's child die? It still makes me cry to think on it. I wanted to crumble to the floor. But the Lord gave my girl some kind of special grace to endure till the end with an amazing strength of faith. I think angels were ministering to her in those final days.

I did not want to believe she was actually dying. Instead, I held out hope she would live. I believed up until the last minute that God would heal her. If ever there was a time for God to show what He is capable of, it was then. There were so many people watching, waiting and praying for a miracle. I knew He *could* do it and I thought He *would* do it. But, for His own reasons He chose not to. Pneumonia had set in as her body lacked the white cells vital for fighting off infection. Our good friend Rob Lane, a retired oncologist, said she was in the waiting room of heaven and we should let her go. In the end we had to release her to go home to the Lord. She breathed her last breath and that was it. There was no miracle - at least as far as earthly eyes could see.

Losing her at such a young age does not make sense to us. Nor does it make God seem very good or loving. Yet, despite the mental wrestling I engage in at times with Him, in my core I know He is still those things. If I was Him, I would have done things differently. I thought this was a chance for Him to show His power so people could see and believe. But He did not choose to work that way.

Jesus said, "Unless a seed falls to the ground and dies it cannot bear fruit" (John 12:24). If my daughter had to fall to the ground and die, I want there to be some fruit. I want for her suffering, and mine, to make sense. Yes, Karina did die, but it was only the shell housing her spirit which was freed in that instant to live on with Jesus. It is because of this truth that I want to tell her story. Jesus Christ gave

Karina hope as she faced death. It was His peace and love that gave her the courage to live fully till the end, confident He would be there to meet her the moment she passed from this life to the next. She did not waiver in this belief, for over the course of her brief 19 years on earth a rock solid foundation of faith had been built and tested.

Karina held to this tried and true fact: the God of the Bible is a God of hope and love despite what happens in life. Despite the pain, the hurt, and the agonizing separation of death, Jesus Christ is the real deal. This is my truth as well, the anchor that holds me in the storm of my loss. Though ultimately He did not answer my prayer in the way I would have liked, He still showed His unfailing love to us over and over through many other answers and miracles, both large and small. I know He is carrying us, and I trust in His ultimate plan.

I hope you will be encouraged as you read our story. My greatest desire is that you will catch a glimpse of Jesus Christ and His amazing love for you and trust Him as the anchor of your soul. I know this would be Karina's heartfelt wish as well. She would not be content with a story told simply about her, or her battle with cancer. She would want it to highlight the HOPE she had in Christ. A hope that is available to all. A hope that holds like an anchor amid the roughest seas and the toughest storms one can ever encounter.

Following Karina's memorial service, we received the most touching letter from missionary friends, Brit and Gayle Hemphill. Although they live and minister in Papua New Guinea, thousands of miles away from Gig Harbor, ironically, they were in the states just at the time of Karina's service. We have known each other as adults for years, but they did not know Karina well and were left only with the observations made of meeting her once a few years prior and the things shared at her memorial. In his letter Brit wrote:

"As I was listening and learning more about Karina at the service, Amy Carmichael repeatedly came to mind. Amy is a hero of mine; one of the people whose life God used mightily to help shape me for overseas missions. Oswald Chambers would have described Amy as 'abandoned to God.' Her story told by Elisabeth Elliot in *A Chance to Die,* is still one of my favorite books…did Karina happen to read it at some point?…In pondering this more since the service I think Amy and Karina would have gotten on well together as young women, maybe even become kindred spirits. I'm sure they have now crossed paths."

Little did Brit know Karina *had* read *A Chance to Die* the summer before her death, while on *Epiphany*. It is the biography of Amy Carmichael, a young Irish woman who gave up a life of privilege in her homeland to minister to the poorest of the poor in the slums of India. Karina found it a deeply meaningful book and could not put it down. In fact, with urgency she had said to me, "Mom, you *have* to read this book!" I was unfamiliar with Amy Carmichael's life, but Karina was clearly inspired by this little-known woman who lived over a hundred years ago. Amy's life of complete surrender to the purpose of God inspired Karina greatly. Since the book is somewhat obsolete, I was amazed Brit would mention it and very touched he saw a resemblance in the lives of these two young women. Like young Amy, Karina knew a reality that escapes most of us as we busy ourselves with the trivial. This life is but a vapor, in an instant, it can be over. Karina had faced death twice: How little did we know less than a year later, as a freshman in college, she would face it again. This time, it would win, or so it seemed.

Brit's letter also included a poem by Henry Van Dyke* that offered immediate comfort. We often assume death is the end, but this poem describes it more as the beginning...the dawn rather than the dusk:

I am standing upon the seashore. A ship at my side spreads her white sails to the morning breeze and starts for the blue ocean. She is an object of beauty and strength. I stand and watch her until at length she hangs like a speck of white cloud just where the sun and sky come to mingle with each other.

Then someone at my side says, "There she is gone!"

Gone where?

Gone from my sight--that is all.

She is just as large in mast and hull and spar as she was when she left my side and just as able to bear her load of living freight to her destined port.

Her diminished size is in me, not in her.

And just at the moment when someone at my side says, "There she is gone!" There are other eyes watching her coming, and other voices ready to take up the glad shout:

"Here she comes!"

And that is dying.

Brit ended his letter by saying, "I imagine Jesus being in the front of the group taking up the glad shout!"

And I agree. For now, she is gone from my sight. That is all.

*Henry Van Dyke was a pastor, educator, and avid writer living in Pennsylvania in the late 1800's. His most famous work is the hymn "Joyful, Joyful We Adore Thee" sung to the tune of Beethoven's "Ode to Joy." Van Dyke remained deeply committed to his faith and hope in Jesus Christ amid the pain of losing his two older children. It is possible, this poem was written about their passing.

Gone from My Sight --- that is all.

A sketch by Katie.

Our Special Treasure, Karina Jean.

A sketch by Katie for Karina.

Dedicated
to
my sister, Karina
my
Best friend

best bro

daddys girl

Chapter 2: Young Life and Malibu

Once I had answered the voice I heard at age twelve and begun my friendship with Jesus, my greatest desire was to know Christ and make Him known. Young Life awakened my husband Ron and I to the reality of having a vibrant and growing relationship with Jesus. Through Young Life, we learned how to cultivate that relationship. Sharing this simple good news of Jesus with others became our passion, and Young Life provided the perfect opportunity. Our involvement over the years, first as volunteer leaders, then with Ron in various Staff positions, has been the bedrock of our life together. Karina was born into this environment and was continually exposed to the Bible studies, youth activities, and summer camp experiences. Our love for Young Life was shared by Karina as well, and our story, along with hers, starts with this awesome organization which is near and dear to each of us.

Young Life was begun in 1941 by an enthusiastic young pastor named Jim Rayburn. He had been raised in a very stoic and legalistic Presbyterian home by well-meaning religious parents. Like many Christians in mainstream churches, they possessed biblical head knowledge, yet lacked the heart of compassion, mercy, and grace. They presented God as a harsh, judgmental figure. Who would want to be friends with that kind of God, let alone trust Him with their life? While Jim held to the core beliefs of his parents, he had come to experience the grace, love, and freedom of knowing Jesus in a personal way. He knew if kids could experience this for themselves, they would want to know Jesus too. He knew Christ was the best thing to happen in his life, but he also realized many will never listen, let alone believe, the message of God's love, because the packaging is all wrong. In fact, he held as his motto: *It is a sin to bore kids with the gospel.* He was determined to find a better way of capturing the interest of teens and sharing the good news of Jesus Christ. He felt traditional Sunday church services held little appeal to modern teenagers and decided another day of the week, an evening at that, would be a better option. Rather than a church building associated with everything boring and irrelevant to most teenagers, Jim developed the idea of meeting in homes and community centers for what he named Young Life Club. It became the perfect setting where Jim, ever enthusiastic, could talk to teens in their language and in such a way they heard and understood the message of Jesus Christ like never before. Kids were drawn to his warm, fun, adventurous spirit. He had an easy way of connecting with them and of earning their trust and respect. He shared, through his own life, the love of Christ, and kids responded to both him and the good news of Christ in great numbers.

Summer camps also became a big part of the Young Life experience. Jim loved the outdoors and wanted to share that love with kids. He felt nature was a great conduit into understanding the truth of the Creator. Jim also saw how busy were the lives of teenagers, providing a constant distraction from thinking about anything deep or important. Camps were a way to get kids away from all the stresses of their lives - school, jobs, boyfriends and girlfriends, conflicted homes - and give them an unforgettable outdoor experience intermingled with caring adults, extreme fun, deeply personal testimonies, and teachings about Jesus Christ. The first camps were in Colorado and included beautiful mountain top getaways. Many were high class resorts that had gone bankrupt. With a vision for transforming them into amazing teen camps, he would often buy these for a fraction of the original listed price. His own board of directors could hardly believe how it would happen, but Jim was a visionary, and a man of deep faith. He felt God could, and would, do anything. Many camps he established are still in operation today, including the one near and dear to us as a family, Malibu, in British Columbia. Malibu is one of the gems of the Young Life organization, and as Young Life leaders and volunteers our family has had the privilege of spending time there nearly every summer. To Karina, it was the best place on earth.

Young Life continues to thrive in communities around the nation using both paid staff and volunteers. As Young Life staff, Ron and I followed the kind of "formula" Jim advocated years before. There are basically three layers to Young Life. The first is fun, the next is friendship, and the final is faith. Young Life provides kids with a weekly night of good, safe, fun, and for many kids, this is all it ever becomes. But the main goal is to build friendships in hopes of influencing them in their faith journey. We planned social times for teens in the community, befriended them, and welcomed them into our home for deeper discussions on faith and the Bible. Of course, from the very beginning of her life Karina was always in the middle of this happy chaos.

Ron grew up in Tacoma, Washington, as the eldest of one brother and one sister. Like me, he was raised in the Lutheran Church, but Young Life became the true catalyst for spiritual growth in his life. This is where he came to understand the Christian faith and decided to live his life entirely for the Lord. The same was true for me. I had first said "yes" to Christ at that Seattle concert, and it was through the teaching of my older sister, Laurie, who became the church youth group leader when I was in junior high, that my faith really took root. But Young Life provided the fertile ground for my growth in the Lord during my high school years. It quickly attracted me and became the place where my understanding of who Christ was and what He did for me was deepened. As teenagers, Ron and I were ideal candidates for Young Life.

Chapter 3: Inlet Love

The first time I met Ron he was working on staff for Young Life. It was at a leadership camp I attended as a college student. He was up front and had a charismatic stage presence along with a great speaking ability. I also found him to be very handsome. Since he was clearly older I assumed he was married and thought his wife must be one lucky lady. I did not know then that he was actually a single guy, and that one day, I would end up being the "lucky lady."

He had begun his college career at Fort Steilacoom Community College outside Tacoma. Even then, as a young man he was very entrepreneurial and excelled in his business classes. He was also running Young Life groups at Curtis High school in south Tacoma. Later, he transferred to Western Washington University in Bellingham where he did very well as a marketing and communications major. Upon graduation he was offered a lucrative job with very good pay, but the Lord had laid on his heart to be involved with Young Life full-time. Because of this he turned down the job. The offer came again, and again he turned it down. After a third offer with the same response, the baffled employer demanded to know what else was so attractive that Ron would turn down such an amazing opportunity. Although it may not have made sense to some people, at that time in his life, Ron was determined to live out the Jim Rayburn legacy. He heard the call and surrendered it all to make Christ known, submitting to the plan God had for him.

Words from a biography about Jim Rayburn, best explain this calling:

"Our young people today...are waiting for someone to care about them....Jim was calling sharp young men and women to sacrifice...to be suffering servants and to take up the cross....he knew there wasn't any other way to get the job done. What we largely have today is a cross-less faith. Many people don't want to pay the price anymore. The irony is that the sharpest young men and women, tomorrow's generation of leaders, are looking for the kind of risk-it-all commitment that Jim called his people to in the first place."

It was not that the job Ron had been offered was wrong in itself, but it would not have been right for Ron since he truly felt the Lord leading him to full-time ministry. Thus he joined Young Life's staff with its meager pay and moved to Gig Harbor, where he became the part-time area director for Peninsula High School and youth director at a local church the rest of the time. He loved living in this waterside community in a cabin on the beach with a group of guys. Every day would begin with water skiing in the bay to the breath-taking backdrop of Mount Rainier. When he was asked to move to Snohomish to build up the Young Life there, it was a difficult decision. He knew he would have to leave a place he loved, but he also desired to please the Lord. Out of obedience he moved and together with his friend, Bill Duppenthaler, they built up the greater Snohomish/Everett Young Life group to become one of the largest in the nation.

During the time he was advancing his Young Life career I was growing up in North Seattle, one in a set of identical twins. We are the youngest out of two older sisters and an older brother. I was a busy high school student involved with sports and extra-curricular activities like Young Life. In the summer, however, I was always too busy to attend Malibu, the dream of most Young Life kids. It was not until the summer following my high school graduation that I was finally able to go. It was a most inspiring time. I had attended many different summer camps, but there is something very special about Malibu.

Jim Rayburn must have felt the magic of the area himself when he ventured up the stunning Princess Louisa inlet for the first time. He immediately set his sights on claiming Malibu for the Lord's purposes. The camp, originally built to lure Hollywood stars to the Northwest, is built at the mouth of the inlet overlooking the rapids. Surrounded by jagged rock faced mountains, deep blue water and peaceful shoreline, it is truly breathtaking. Jim knew it was the kind of place where kids from all over the region would encounter the handiwork of the Creator. With grand faith he dared to believe Young Life could make the purchase, and shortly thereafter his dream became reality.

Psalm 19: 1-2 says:

"The heavens declare the glory of God; the skies proclaim the work of his hands, day after day they pour forth speech and night after night they display knowledge."

This is certainly true of Malibu. It serves as a visual aid to the glory of God. From the mountain peaks surrounding the misty forest to the star studded night sky, one cannot stand in such a place without being humbled. The creation speaks day and night of the glory and majesty of God. To think it was this very God who had reached out to mankind through the person of His son, Jesus! I was hooked and knew that somehow, someway I wanted to return to Malibu. I wanted to be a part of sharing the awesome love of Jesus Christ with kids and teens for the rest of my life. It was a life-changing moment.

That autumn I attended the University of Washington, and the following summer I worked as a counselor at Camp Arnold, a Salvation Army camp in Eatonville. I knew then I wanted to give more time to ministry. I had entered the University of Washington as part of the crew team, but midway through my second year, I felt the calling from the previous summer to be involved full-time in youth ministry. I made the pivotal choice to quit crew and become a Young Life leader which would allow me to be involved year round. I became a leader at Roosevelt High School where I mentored kids in their faith during the school year and accompanied them to Malibu during the summer. I was a leader for the next four years.

Since I also loved small children, I became an intern at University Presbyterian Church for two summers and also served as a Sunday school teacher during the year. I loved working with kids and teenagers alike, and a new dream developed of becoming a full-time children's ministry director. As an intern at what is known as "U Pres," I was mentored by some awe-inspiring older Christians.

During this time I was introduced to Henrietta Mears through her book *Dream Big*. Her writings were deeply instrumental in my spiritual development. Mears was a simple school teacher in the 1940's who had a passion for teaching kids and young adults the good news of Jesus. From her home in Hollywood, she was able to influence many college students, young adults, and Hollywood stars who were seeking spiritual understanding in life. She had a passion for reading, teaching and encouraging others to study the Bible. If people would simply read the Bible with an open mind, asking God to reveal its message, she reasoned they would see and understand the grand story of redemption woven within its pages. She longed for people to come to an understanding of this "divine generosity." Mears also had a burning desire to develop young people into strong spiritual leaders. I discovered she had been the catalyst in the lives of some great Christian leaders of our time such as Billy Graham; Bill Bright, who founded Campus Crusade for Christ; and young Jim Rayburn, who went on to found Young Life. Her testimony and passion evoked a desire in me to be sold out as a witness for Christ.

Throughout these years Ron and I would see each other at various Young Life leadership events. By then I was a volunteer leader at Roosevelt high school, and he was on staff in Snohomish. To my surprise, I discovered he was not married and my interest was sparked. But I was also a busy college student, and he was a busy Young Life Staffer. A few years passed before we finally connected on the *Malibu Princess*, the boat which originally ferried campers up the inlet to the camp. We were on the way home from a leadership retreat. I had not seen him much while there, but en route home on the *Princess*, we found ourselves talking nonstop the entire eight hour boat ride. It is called "inlet love" by those in the Malibu circle. Surrounded by the beauty of the inlet, the time flew as we discovered our common Lutheran backgrounds, shared love of the Lord, and passion for telling teens about the good news of Jesus Christ. When we parted I was hoping to meet "that Ron Robertson guy" again, but we went the whole summer without seeing each other. I had just graduated from the University of Washington with a degree in Speech and Hearing Sciences with a teaching certificate. My first job teaching fourth graders would start that September. Although no new teacher in their right mind would continue extracurricular activities during their first year, I kept my volunteer position as a Young Life leader in hopes of seeing Ron again. Sure enough that autumn found us together at another leadership event, and our relationship took off. Five months later, he proposed and we were married August 14, 1987.

Opposite page:

WEDDING ANNIVERSARY POSTCARD FROM
KARINA TO MOM AND DAD

This is where it all began.
Have a very happy anniversary!!!
Love, Karina XOXO

Front of postcard, opposite (boat): Painting of the Malibu
Princess, where Ron and Katie met when they were
twenty eight and twenty three years old on their way
home from a leadership retreat at Malibu. The boat is
the only way other than seaplane or water taxi to get to
Malibu. At that time, the boat left from Vancouver, and
it was an eight hour boat ride. Now, it leaves from
Egmont and takes only three hours.

Katie says: "We were sitting on the top deck for the
whole trip home. He had sat their purposefully so he
could get to know me. I was thrilled, and hoped I would
see him again."

Lower photo, opposite page: Katie and Ron, on their
wedding day, August 14, 1987.

Sketch by Katie.

"Malibu Princess". Malibu Club. British Columbia. Canada

This is were it all began. Have a very happy anniversary!!!

Love,
Karina xoxo

To Mom & Dad

Chapter 4: Our Love of Boating

For our honeymoon, Ron and I went on a 10 day sailing trip around the San Juan Islands. It was then we discovered the historic seaside town of Roche Harbor together. Before that, I had never even been to these breathtaking islands in the North Puget Sound near Canada. Ron had grown up taking small skiffs around the shores of the south sound, but he learned how to sail when he was the area director in Snohomish. His committee chairman, John Carlson, owned a 39 ft C & C sailboat called the *Mirage,* which was moored in Everett. Knowing Ron loved the water, John would often take Ron out sailing, teaching him everything he knew. In fact, John would often call Ron at the office asking him to meet at the yacht club to go over committee notes, which was actually code for "let's go sailing."

Ron wanted to share his love of the sea with me and borrowed the boat for our honeymoon. It was a wonderful trip. We especially fell in love with the idyllic resort of Roche Harbor. With its peaceful gardens, historic buildings and quiet marina it quickly become a favorite family destination and a special place to Karina as well. This trip also cemented our love of boating and planted within us the dream of owning our own boat.

The beginning years of our marriage were spent living in Snohomish and leading Young Life together at Snohomish high school, where Ron was the area director. Although we loved our work there, Ron's dream and desire was always to be near the water again. He loved boating and had a vision of starting up a sailboat ministry and using it to bring teens along for sailing adventures. "Sailing Beyond" had once been a part of Young Life, and Ron hoped to revive this venture. He spent many hours thinking about the kind of boat that would be right for such a ministry and finally decided on the McGreagor 65, a sleek fiberglass sailboat durable for kids. Shortly thereafter, my high school friend, Nancy (Newbould) Helms, came to visit us. She happened to gaze upon Ron's sailing magazine open on our table to a photo of the very boat he desired.

"Oh!" she exclaimed, "My friend's dad has a boat just like that in Tacoma if you want to see it."

Ron, of course, jumped at the chance. Despite the December chill, the very next day found us trekking to Tacoma to see the boat. As we viewed the vessel and met the skipper, Phil Roth, Ron shared his dream of a teen sailing ministry and his interest in obtaining a similar boat. Working for Young Life would never allow us the income to obtain a boat like this, but in the spirit of Jim Rayburn, Ron held to his vision. He did not know how to make it happen, but we prayed that God would work out the details.

Amazingly, a few months later, in April, Ron got a call from Phil. Phil said he had been thinking and praying about Ron's idea all winter and felt the Lord was leading him to offer his boat with himself as skipper to aid Ron's dream. We were in awe of this answer to our prayers. That next summer "Sail Challenge" began. We operated out of Everett and Anacortes taking Young Life kids on outings. Being on the water gave them a chance to learn about boating, but more importantly, it was a time for them to think more deeply about faith. Nature is often the best conduit for contemplating God since the obligations of daily life can be a real distraction. On the water, kids had a chance to experience the serenity of the Puget Sound and the challenge of sailing. They loved being with us, and we in turn greatly enjoyed being with kids teaching them about boating and God's amazing love.

Phil devoted the last few years of his life to selflessly aiding various boating trips. He willingly gave of his time, expertise, and sailboat for Ron's area as well as other Young Life groups and churches desiring to offer kids such experiences. We were deeply touched by his generosity, and by the way God, once again, showed His attention to our dreams and provided the means to make it happen.

By this time, Karina had been born and she and I went happily along on these adventures. As our family grew, the kids each developed sea legs and loved being on the boat, sailing to favorite places, and playing in and on the water. We all shared a love of sea life in the Northwest. Being on the boat together offered us precious family time away from the obligations of home and work. The waterways of the Puget Sound and British Columbia offer the breathtaking beauty of snow-capped mountains and dense green forests which plummet to meet the deep blue sea. The views filled us with tranquility and calm in the midst of our hectic lives. Boating quickly became a favorite family activity, with Roche Harbor and Malibu being our most cherished destinations.

Top photo opposite : Karina, Annika, and Erik on the bow of
our boat heading in to Young Life's camp Malibu in
Princess Louisa Inlet, British Columbia.

Bottom photo: Our family on the mainstreet boardwalk
at Malibu. The highlight of our annual summer boating
trips was arriving at our favorite destination, Malibu. We
would always anchor in the inlet and then dinghy in for a
daily visit to Malibu. We were all smitten by the beauty of the
place and the feeling of God's presence.

All of the photos of boating in the book are of Princess
Louisa Inlet (including Malibu and Chatterbox Falls),
and Roche Harbor, San Juan Island.

Sketch by Katie of the kids on the bow, boating into Malibu.

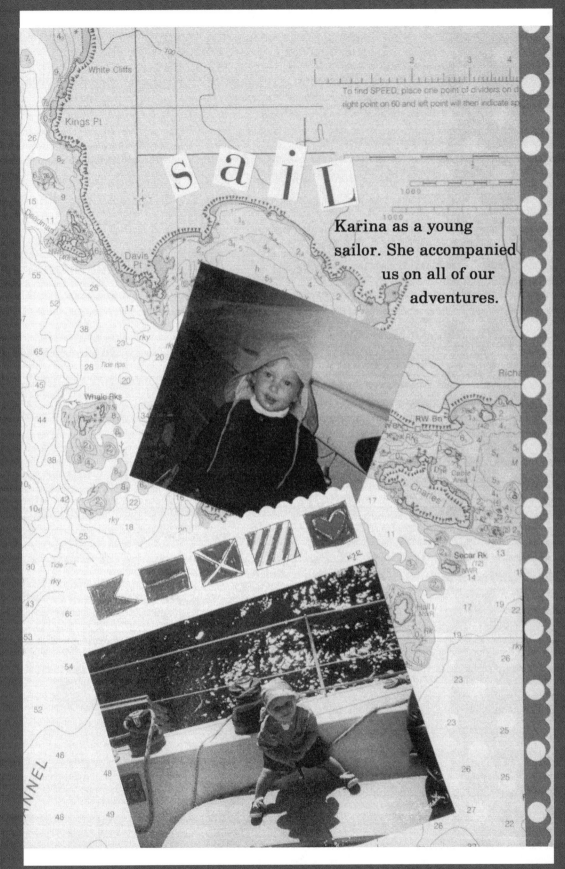

sail

Karina as a young sailor. She accompanied us on all of our adventures.

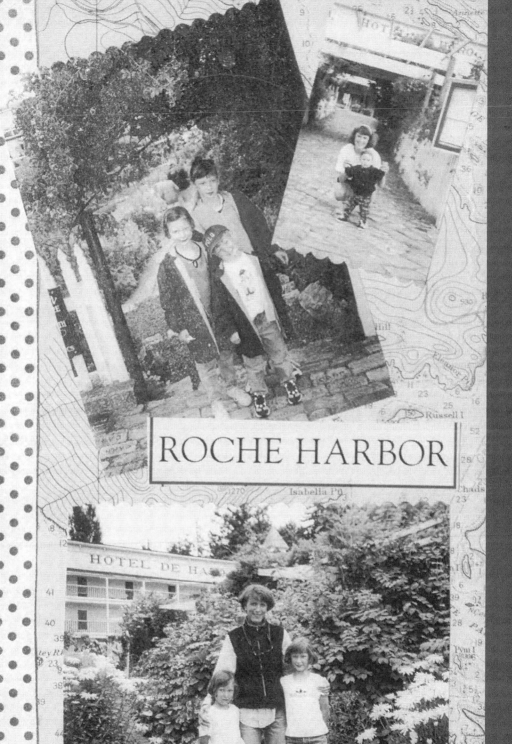

ROCHE HARBOR

Chapter 5: Anchored at Home

It was an exciting time when I found out I was pregnant with our first baby. Within the first four months of the pregnancy both my sisters also became pregnant. However, in the midst of shared joy, we also experienced shared sorrow. Our mom was diagnosed with breast cancer. My mom, Jean, would survive that diagnosis and live another twelve wonderful years. In fact, she, who would become Karina's namesake, became a source of great inspiration to our daughter in the years ahead. Karina would observe the strong faith of her "grammie" Jean and be comforted and encouraged in her own battle with cancer.

I thought for sure Karina would be a boy and picked out all unisex clothes as well as a name for a boy. On September 6, 1990, I was induced and it was like a party in the room with my family surrounding me. When they announced it was a girl I cried with joy. It was the happiest day of my life. I thought, *I could have ten boys and still be content since I have my girl.*

I had to go back to teaching after four months, which was especially difficult. The grandmas helped out, and Karina would also hang out with Ron quite a lot. As a Young Life staff person, he enjoyed a very flexible schedule and could easily spend time with her. They grew to be very good buddies.

I realized pretty quickly the difficulty of juggling the needs of my baby with the demands of my teaching job. That first year back in the classroom after Karina was born was so stressful. Although I was only working part-time, a teacher's work is never really done. I knew my income was needed at home, but at the same time, I really missed not being with Karina. I did not feel I had a lot of money-making skills other than teaching so one day I prayed: "Lord, there are two things I can do, one is draw and the other is teach piano, but I don't have a piano. If there is any way you can work with that, I sure would love to stay home with Karina." Then, I waited.

The next week, out of the blue, our long-time friends, John and Jan Carlson, called and asked if we could store their piano. I was elated. God had provided the means whereby I could have an income as a stay-at-home mom as well as be with my baby. While Karina napped I was able to have a few piano students a day. It was a perfect arrangement and I thanked God for making this happen. It was just one of those seemingly small but important requests He orchestrated for me in a way I could not have imagined. That is the kind of God I kept discovering over and over again. It's not that He is a Santa Claus, giving us everything on our list. But like a caring parent, He is there to help when we are hitting a dead end and do not know what to do. I had learned that part of having a friendship with God meant I could seek Him whenever faced with a dilemma I did not know how to solve. He had convinced me of His care and concern for every area of my life. Asking Him for help became second nature. In fact, I often quoted I Peter 5:7 to little Karina:

"Cast **all** your cares upon Him, for He cares about you."

I taught her that casting *all* of your cares means telling Him everything that concerns us: big or little, important or seemingly insignificant. He cares about us. This teaching truly sunk deep into her spirit and became second nature to her as well. When faced with cancer, the biggest scare ever, she did what she had learned to do with all of the little scares…cast them on Him for she knew He cared for her.

On February 11, 1993, when Karina was two and a half, her baby sister Annika joined our family. I was ecstatic to have two girls. Karina Jean and Annika Joy quickly became the best of friends. They spent hours together as little girls playing with dolls, their favorite being American Girl and Barbie dolls, and would create elaborate scenarios such as their dolls attending boarding school. Together they would also play "dress up" and "house" in their little kitchen. At Karina's initiative they set up a school and library with her in charge. In fact, Annika was the first girl in her class to read and be able to sign her name in cursive thanks to Karina's tutoring. They always shared their bedroom. Even after we moved into our current house and built two beautiful new bedrooms, they continued to more or less live together in one room. Of course, those early years with two small children were busy as every mom knows, but my life was really about to get crazy.

With Karina almost four and Annika almost two, I became pregnant again and May 4, 1995, brought the blessing of our son, Erik James. It was especially chaotic as our family was undergoing many changes. I was thinking of returning to my teaching career and Ron had accepted a job in Planned Giving for Young Life Development. This job change meant we could live anywhere in the Northwest, and Ron jumped at the chance to return to Gig Harbor.

Phil Roth, the kind older man who had so generously given us use of his sailboat years earlier, had a piece of property that had been sitting on the market in Gig Harbor for two years. It was not an attractive lot, but it sat on a hill overlooking Shaw's Cove, one of the many inlets of the south Puget Sound. Given its beach access, it was our dream location. When we went to view it, Phil suggested if Ron stood on the roof of a little shed on the property, he would be able to see Mt. Rainier. It took some vision, but we realized a house would offer these same views. We were so blessed to be offered this land at a very reasonable price and made plans to build our home.

In addition to Ron's job change, the house building project, and a new baby, I had begun seeking the continuing education credits needed to renew my teaching certificate. We had just moved from Snohomish and were renting a house in Gig Harbor. While it was exciting to be building a new house, we were discovering many complicated issues with the property, and the accumulating stress began to wear on me. Things came to a head immediately following Erik's birth. I was thrilled to become the mother of a son but did not feel myself. I became anxious about many things: losing sleep, nursing Erik, and getting things done.

Most women recover from childbirth without a problem, so it is difficult to fully describe the variety of baffling feelings associated with post-partum depression. For me, it felt like being swallowed up in a valley of anxiety and despair. So much was going on in our life that I started to feel completely out of control. On the outside my life looked perfect. I had an adorable baby boy with blue eyes and blonde curls and two sweet little girls. We had been blessed with prime Gig Harbor property for a house, and my husband was growing into a new and exciting career. Inside, however, I felt completely desperate and hopeless. The fact things looked so great on the outside only added to my despair, for I could not talk myself out of these anxious feelings. I began to question my faith, *Lord where **are** you? Have you forgotten me?*

My sense of hopelessness was further compounded by a counselor who did not understand and left me feeling I was forever stuck in this abyss. Needless to say, this was a crisis both emotionally and spiritually. I was left feeling entirely alone with no support, no resources, and very little hope. Two things helped me find my bearing during this very difficult and frightening time.

Firstly, I forced myself to attend my weekly women's Bible study, not because I felt the least bit close to God, but because I knew He was all I had even though I could not feel Him at the moment. During one morning study, I was sitting in the group nursing Erik when it came my turn to read. As I turned to Isaiah 49:15 and read the words out loud, I was shocked by their relevance:

"Can a mother forget the baby at her breast and have no compassion on the child she has born? Though she may forget, I will never forget you!"

I knew God was speaking directly to me through that scripture, especially since the verse was being graphically and literally illustrated at that very moment. God the Father was reminding me I was not a forgotten child. He was with me in this confusing time. That promise gave me renewed strength and hope. I knew for certain I was not alone and He would get me through this crisis. This was truly an anchoring moment in my faith. When I look back now, I realize He allowed this time of suffering to make me stronger in my reliance on Him and His promises. While I would not want to repeat that experience, at the same time, I am grateful for what it taught me: His faithfulness and presence reaches even into our most confusing depths and darkest hours.

A second strong source of comfort came from the classic Christian book *Hinds Feet on High Places* by Hannah Hurnard. Written as an allegory, the story is about a deer named "Much Afraid" who follows the voice of her loving shepherd and rises out of the Valley of Fear to the heights above. This simple story gave me practical comfort and inspired me to listen to the reassuring voice of my shepherd rather than my illogical feelings. This book became another favorite spiritual resource and I used the child's version to teach Karina the reality of having a friend like Jesus to lead us out of our personal valleys of fear.

During this time, I was led to follow the instruction of Philippians 4:8, 9:

"Whatever is true, whatever is noble, whatever is right, whatever is pure, whatever is lovely, whatever is admirable - if anything is excellent or praiseworthy - think about such things. Whatever you have learned or received or heard from me, or seen in me - put it into practice. And the God of peace will be with you."

I determined to focus on what I knew to be true rather than on my confusing feelings which could easily lead me astray: God loved me and He was there for me. He had a plan for me and would never leave me. He always hears me.

Although it took over a year, little by little I began to crawl out of my own valley of fear. The fog lifted, the sun began to shine anew and with our house complete we moved in and continued the daily task of raising kids.

Photo opposite: newborn Karina.

"Your Parents' Thoughts" From Karina's Baby Book, by Katie

Karina you are more wonderful than I could have ever imagined! You truly are a blessing to me! It is amazing how well formed you are...you are a beautiful little baby! I am <u>so</u> excited to be your mother! I want to share a life full of joy with you and teach you of God's love! God has a special plan for your life. I love you <u>so</u> much!

Sketch by Katie of baby Karina in her pool.

Your Parents' Thoughts

Mother _Karina you are more wonderful than I could have ever imagined! You truly are a blessing to me! It is amazing how well formed you are ··· you are a beautiful little baby! I am so excited to be your mother! I want to share a life full of joy with you and teach you of God's love! God has a special plan for your life ☺ I love you so much!_

Father _____

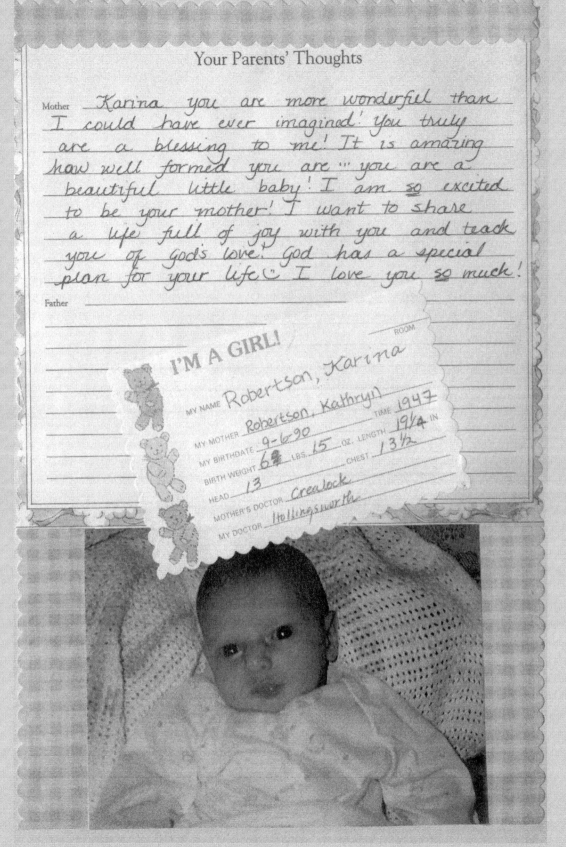

I'M A GIRL!

ROOM _____

MY NAME _Robertson, Karina_

MY MOTHER _Robertson, Kathryn_

MY BIRTHDATE _9-6-90_   TIME _1947_

BIRTH WEIGHT _6_ LBS. _15_ OZ. LENGTH _19¼_ IN

HEAD _13_   CHEST _13½_

MOTHER'S DOCTOR _Crealock_

MY DOCTOR _Hollingsworth_

47

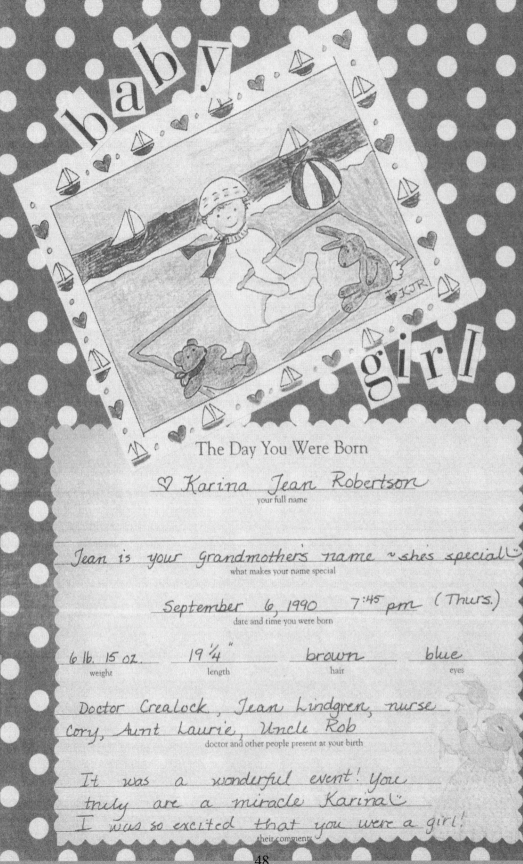

baby

girl

The Day You Were Born

♡ Karina Jean Robertson
your full name

Jean is your Grandmother's name ~ she's special ♡
what makes your name special

September 6, 1990   7:45 pm   (Thurs.)
date and time you were born

6 lb. 15 oz.   19 ¼ "   brown   blue
weight   length   hair   eyes

Doctor Crealock, Jean Lindgren, nurse
Cory, Aunt Laurie, Uncle Rob
doctor and other people present at your birth

It was a wonderful event! You
truly are a miracle Karina ♡
I was so excited that you were a girl!
their comments

48

as much as to say that they don't want her to get lost, and
may be recognized by ma...   Hurry up! Don't t...
feet inward; a well...   ...g turns his feet out...
much as possi...   ...d mother. Look, l...
Now be...

...t them and sa...
...at lot too; ...
...hat one D...

...m, and ...

...is d...

...cked.
...has," said ...
...e all fine, exc...
...h h...

...ing's
"...beau...an
think ...will gr...   ...maller
He has lain to...   ...hot rece...
right shape."   ...le one's ...
smoothed his ...   ...is a dra...
therefore it d...   ...e will bec...
strong and f...
"The ...   ...said the ol...

A Quote About Motherhood that Inspired Katie as a Young Mother

There is no nobler career than that of motherhood at its best. There are no possibilities greater, and in no other sphere does failure bring more serious penalties. With what diligence then should she prepare herself for such a task. If the mechanic who is to work with "things" must study at technical school, if the doctor into whose skilled hands will be entrusted human lives must go to medical school...how much more should the mother who is fashioning the souls of men and women of tomorrow learn at the highest of all schools and from the Master-Sculptor Himself, God. To attempt this task unprepared and untrained is tragic, and its results affect generations to come. On the other hand, there is no higher height to which humanity can attain than that occupied by a converted, heaven-inspired, PRAYING mother.

Anonymous

Katie and little Karina reading together.

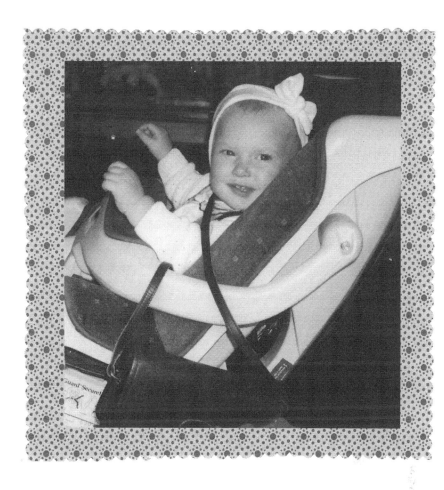

Photo: Karina at nine months old.

When Karina was a little girl, she loved to hear the story of her lost white headband. When Karina was nine months old, we were shopping at Costco together. She was riding in a backpack, wearing her white headband. When we left, I noticed it was gone. It was lost somewhere in Costco. I quickly searched the store, and found nothing. Frustrated, and knowing it was there, I asked the Lord with his all-seeing eyes to help me find it. I looked down, and there it was, under a shelf! Karina loved this story because it demonstrated how God listens to everything.

Opposite page: a poem written by Karina for Annika.

A LITTLE SISTER

A little sister is a small little friend
who wants to be like you in every way.
She is fun to be with. I love her in
every way. She is my good friend. She
is the best out of the rest. I think she is
the best. I love her very much!

Left photo: Ron, Karina, and baby Annika.
Right photo: Katie, Karina and baby Annika.

The family at camp Malibu. Sketch by Katie.

A Little Sister

A little sister is a small little friend. Who wants to be like you in every way.

She is fun to be with. I love her in every way. She is my good friend. She is the best out of the rest. I think she is the best. I love her very much!

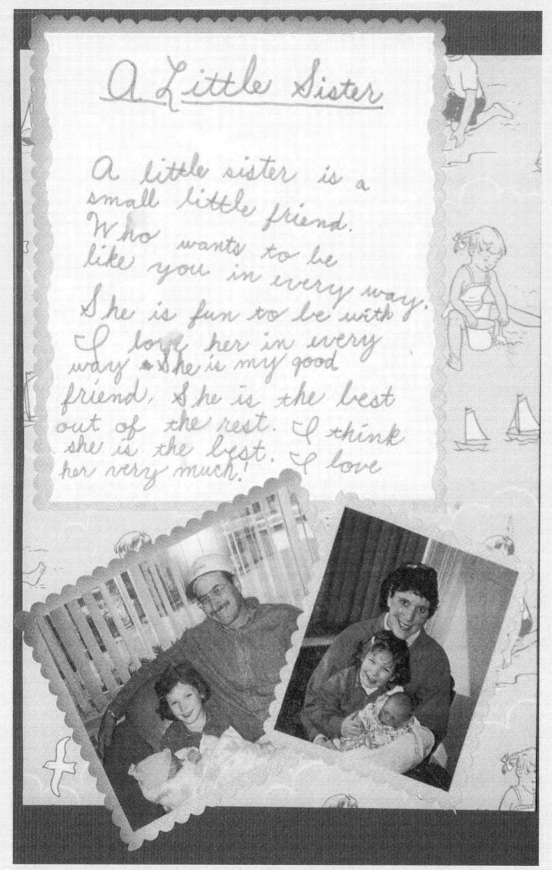

Picture on opposite page:

I am your sister...

...and you are my friend.

A painting by Jesse Wilcox Smith which seemed to me
to perfectly capture the life of my young daughters
as they played together on the shores of Puget Sound.

The girls and I used to play making pancakes and crab
soup. They loved building "fairy houses" out of natural
materials in the driftwood. The sisters loved playing
together. Erik, the girls, and I often took beach walks
to look for sand dollars. There was an old wrecked barge up
the beach which we called "the shipwreck." We had a
great time together.

Sketch by Katie.

I am your sister...

...and you are my friend

21 Princess Louisa Inlet. Use Chart 3514 or Chartbook 3312. Princess Louisa Inlet, miles long, is the "holy grail" for cruising pe ple from all over the world. Entered throu Malibu Rapids, the inlet is surrounded mile-high mountains that drop almost cally into 500-foot depths below. En Princess Louisa Inlet is like entering a cathedral. The author Earle Stanley C wrote that no one could see Princes Inlet and remain an atheist. It is o most awesome destinations on r What words can describe this plac superlatives have been used up or jects. *Please observe a no-wake spee wakes bounce off the sides of the inle*

Malibu Club, a Young Life C mer camp for teenagers, is at Princess Louisa Inlet, just ins ids. The kids are welcoming they'll show you around. It's see Malibu Club when you you want a place at the pa box Falls, you'd better g if you leave the park doc day you can tie up at t Malibu Rapids and ta' even see the rapids cal approaches, and time narrow pass perfectly

As you clear Mali Princess Louisa Inlet, you w waterfalls streaming down the mountain

Chapter 6: Epiphany

Throughout the years when the kids were young, before we owned a boat, we chartered a sailboat every summer for vacations on the Puget Sound. Working for Young Life Development meant Ron would seize every opportunity to expose potential donors to the majestic beauty of the Princess Louisa Inlet and the Young Life camp at Malibu. He knew once people experienced the stunning views of the inlet, visited the camp, and saw the impact it had on teens, they would want to invest in it. Thus he would invite boating enthusiasts to accompany us on these summer trips. It became known as the Malibu Yacht Club, and we sailed from Anacortes with Ron as the leader. Our family loved those outings. We would be on the boat two or three weeks at a time enjoying the sea, the sights, and the precious family time. Stops usually included Roche Harbor and often Rosario Resort or Victoria BC, along with other spots on the way to the final destination of Malibu.

Over the course of these summer sailing excursions we began to develop an interest in power boating. A bigger power boat would enable us to travel faster and bring more people along. We started attending boat shows and dreaming, for we had no idea when or if we could afford a boat like this. Along the way we met many interesting people, some of whom have become dear friends. One such couple is Randy and Maureen Crowley, a Mercer Island couple who sold yachts. We first met them and their beautiful 68 ft Westbay Sonship *Epiphany* in 2001. We loved the way they had designed the interior, but the story of the naming of the boat was another amazing coincidence.

Being from California, they had boated up one summer to none other than Princess Louisa Inlet. Boaters from southern California enjoy year round warmth and beautiful coast line, but it is no visual comparison to boating in the Northwest. As they powered along the inlets of British Columbia they found the rugged peaks and sparkling waters breathtaking. In fact, they experienced a personal "epiphany" and decided to move to the Northwest. They were especially touched by the power and majesty of the God who created the stunning beauty of this place. While anchored by Chatterbox Falls at the head of the inlet Maureen happened to read Psalms 29:3-4:

"The voice of the Lord is over the waters; the God of glory thunders, the Lord thunders over the mighty waters."

Just like the time when the scripture I was reading aloud in my women's group was being graphically portrayed by baby Erik on my lap, Maureen saw and heard the verses she was reading illustrated right before her eyes. Chatterbox Falls literally thunders as its icy glacial waters pour off the rocks and tumble to the depths below. It was a moment of keen awareness for her as to the awe and wonder of God.

Our shared experience with an area we also love so much was unbelievable. Even so, at the time, we did not see how we could afford such a nice craft. Time went by and year by year we would see Randy and Maureen and *Epiphany* at the Seattle Boat Show. Every year we loved it more. They were trying to sell it and took it out to the east coast, but it never sold. Much like our first Gig Harbor property, it seemed as if God was reserving this boat just for us. In time, Ron left Young Life to develop his own wealth management firm and group of mutual funds. It was the same line of work in which he was originally offered employment, but turned down, years before. He started the business with one of his former Young Life kids, Gary Price, and it turned out to be a real blessing for us as they did very well. By the winter of 2005, to our great surprise, the financing came together and we became the proud, and very blessed, owners of *Epiphany*. We dedicated the boat for God's purposes and prayed that everyone who stepped on board would have their own "epiphany" and catch a glimpse of the love and grace of God. That first spring we took it out a few times and enjoyed every minute. There is a closeness that develops as a family when forced into tight quarters. Our weeks at home often sent us off in different directions; however, together, on *Epiphany* we were given the chance to reconnect in an atmosphere of beauty and serenity on the water.

We were excited to celebrate Annika's birthday on board over winter break of 2005 and on Memorial Day weekend we went to Roche Harbor. It was during that holiday we met and made acquaintance with another boater who lives on Hunt's Point in Bellevue. Little did we know how significant a role this new friendship would play in our future needs with Karina. Looking back, we would see how the Lord was orchestrating events, including the purchase of this boat, to help us in our most desperate times. It served as yet more evidence of how He loves us and cares for every detail of our lives.

POWERBOATS OVER SAILBOATS,
A PAPER WRITTEN BY KARINA FOR SCHOOL

by Karina, fourth grade

I think powerboats are better than sailboats. They are better because you stay warm and dry, and you have more room. I think most people would rather ride in a powerboat than in a sailboat. One time when my family and I were on a sailboat, it was raining. My dad had to stear outside of the cabin. It was so cold he had to wear all of his coats and he had to hold a cup of coffee. The next time my family and I went boating we chartered a powerboat. For example, it takes two days to get to Roche Harbor by sailboat if you have alot of wind. It takes four hours by powerboat. Powerboats are much faster than sailboats. Sailboats have pretty small motors, but powerboats, on the other hand, have one or two BIG motors. Powerboats are much more comfortable than sailboats. It is pretty hard to stay comfortable on a sailboat with two adults, two kids, and one baby. Those are my reasons why powerboats are better than sailboats.

Karina chose a topic that she loved. We had many boating adventures as a family. It was our favorite family activity. We would go for several weeks each summer and loved being together.

Powerboats Over Sailboats

I think powerboats are better than sailboats. They are better because you stay warm, dry, and you have more room. I think most poeple would rather ride in a powerboats than a sailboat. One time when my family and I were on sailboat it was raining my dad had to strear outside of the cabin he was so cold he had to wear all his coats and he had to hold a cup of coffee. The next time my family and I went boating we chartered a powerboat. For example it takes two days to get to Roche Harbor by sailboat if you have alot of wind. It takes four hours to get by powerboat. Powerboats are much faster than sailboats. Sailboats have pretty small motors, but powerboats on the other hand have one or two BIG motors. Powerboats are much more comfortable than sailboats. It is pretty hard too stay comfortable on a sailboat with two adults, two kids, and one baby. Those are my reasons why powerboats are better than sailboats.

Kevin O.
18

Princess Louisa Society. The Princess Louisa Society was formed to buy and pre-serve the area around Chatterbox Falls for perpetuity. The Society gave the property to BC Parks, but maintains an active role in the ___ of the facilities. Fundraising continues to ___ and develop the facilities at docks ___ area. Annual memberships are $40 ___ Life memberships are $200 U.S. ___ ciety website is www.princess-

Chatterbox Falls,
Princess Louisa
Inlet, British
Columbia.

A mother's treasure
is her daughter.
—Catherine Pulsifer

PRINCESS LOUISA
MARINE PARK

Chatterbox
Falls
Public

Mt Helena
1554

PRINCESS LOUISA
MARINE PARK

Macdonald

PRINCESS LOUISA INLET

PRINCESS LOUISA
MARINE PARK

malibu

Malibu
IR

Malibu Rapids
Inset
Cartouche

Roche Harbor
boating
adventures.

Opposite page: a paper Karina wrote for school.

FAVORITE VACATION
by Karina, fifth grade

My favorite place to go is Malibu, the Young Life camp. The only way to get there is by seaplane or boat. When you get there, it is like entering another world. There are immense mountains surrounding it. I love it there!

There are tons of fun things to do there like swimming in a pool blasted out of rock, or messing around the game room and playing foosball or air hockey. You can also go to the craft cart and make a really cool necklace. You also could go to the Totem Inn and get delicious ice cream. You could also go to the Totem Trader and buy cool stuff or go on a hike. You can go play volleyball, too.

At the end of the day, everyone goes to Club. At Club you sing songs, see a skit, then there's a message. At the end of the week, there is a "say so" when people say they have asked God in their heart.

Sketch by Annika of
the Malibu inner dock.

Favorite Vacation

My favorite place to go is
Malibu, the Young Life camp.
The only way to get there is
by seaplane or boat. When you
get there it is like entering another
world! There are immense mountains
surrounding it. I love it there!
There are tons of fun things
to do there like swimming in
a pool blasted out of rock, or
messing around the game room
and playing foosball or airhockey.
You can also go to the craft cart
and make a really cool necklace.
You also could go the Totem Inn
and get delicious ice cream. You
could also go to the Totem Trader
and buy cool stuff or go on a
hike. You can go play volleyball
too. At the end of the day
everyone goes to Club. At Club
you sing songs, see a skit, then
there's a message. At the end of
the week there is a say so when
people say they have asked God
in their heart.

MALIBU CLUB
•In Canada•

Chapter 7: Anchoring Kids in Faith

Ron and I had dreamed of raising our kids to know and love God. We deeply desired to share our faith in such a way as it would be real for them. We wanted to raise them to understand how they, too, could enter a personal relationship with the living God. Being involved with Young Life provided a great opportunity: time to devote to them, interaction with wonderful people who loved the Lord, and summer adventures at Malibu.

Through these involvements, as well as church, and my teaching the kids at home, we did our best to instill the truth of Jesus Christ into their hearts. Just as I desired to share Christ with other teens, I also knew when I became a parent I wanted to share this simple good news with my kids. As a school teacher, I truly believed in the high calling of being a mom. Parents hold great power for molding and developing the spirits of these little ones entrusted to our care. I wanted to teach my kids everything I knew about the Lord and show them Jesus as a real person. The following verses guided me and helped give me practical ideas for how to do so.

1. Matthew 19:13-14 NIV
"Jesus said: Let the little children come to me and do not hinder them for the kingdom of heaven belongs to such as these."

From these words of Jesus, I learned **a child is never too young to soak up God's love for them.**

2. Deuteronomy 6:6-7
"These commandments I give you today are to be upon your hearts. Impress them on your children. Talk about them when you sit at home and when you walk down the road, when you lie down and when you get up."

This scripture urged me to talk about God wherever I was and whatever I was doing. **I needed to make the most of every opportunity to help my kids see God in the details of life.**

3. James 1:5
"If any of you lack wisdom, he should ask God who gives generously to all without finding fault, and it will be given to him."

This verse told me I could **seek the Lord for wisdom in raising my kids**. If He created my children, then He of all people knew their individual needs and unique personalities. He would help me know best how to parent them.

Although there are many aspects of God which remain a mystery, I knew from my experience that He is also knowable, and deeply desires a personal relationship with each of us. I also knew from working with kids they display a natural curiosity and openness toward Him. I have since had this confirmed by Dr. Thomas, who would become our pediatric oncologist. He has been with many children on their death beds, and what he has observed is truly remarkable. Many of these children, often from no faith background whatsoever, have experiences where they see or hear from Jesus, either directly or via angels. In one instance, Dr. Thomas came into the ICU room of a very sick little six year old girl. She told him matter of fact that angels had just been standing at the foot of her bed. They had told her she would be with Jesus at 6:00 that evening. Sure enough, later that day, she passed away.

These stories, as well as my own experience with children, convinced me of the need to tell kids the good news of Christ. When Jesus said we must become like little children in order to inherit the kingdom, I think He was talking about the kind of open hearts kids have toward God. Children gravitate to a belief in the Creator, and when they have the gospel explained to them, it makes sense. With Karina, I came to realize kids are like freshly tilled soil just waiting for the good seed to fall. With water and sunshine, they are ready to burst into bloom…and, wow, did she ever bloom!

From a very young age I noticed this curiosity in Karina. She truly caught the vision of and shared our Christian faith. At family gatherings, she would open her Bible, flip a few pages, and then confidently proclaim, "And the Lord God said!" before smacking it shut with a grin. She also loved to line up her dolls and play the part of the teacher giving them mini Bible lessons the way she had seen us do at

Campaigners, our weekly Young Life Bible study group. As leaders, we held the Campaigner's groups in our home and would separate the girls from the boys for more intimate conversation. Campaigner's is the name of the Young Life study group for kids who are interested in learning about the Bible in a deeper way. Often on these evenings while I had the girls in one room and Ron taught the boys in another, baby Karina would crawl back and forth from room to room enjoying the attention. On one particular evening she crawled into the boy's room, sat in the middle of the floor, and tore and ate a piece of the Bible that was lying there. The group of course thought she was one funny baby. I ponder now, looking back, how the incident serves as a vivid visual image of who she was then and grew to be: someone who feasted on the Word and believed in it to the core of her being. I do not believe Karina would have had the fortitude to endure reoccurring cancer and face death with the optimism she did, had it not been for her own deeply anchored faith. From a very early age she lived and breathed the Christian faith we taught her.

Karina had a unique way of integrating this faith into little songs such as one she wrote around age three:

"Jesus, Jesus come into my heart today.
Jesus, Jesus come into my heart to stay.
I love you (clap, clap) I love you (clap, clap)

The simple words are a perfect reflection of her incredibly pure and authentic faith. From a very young age her genuine love and belief in God amazed me. She asked spiritual questions and made observations well beyond her years. She would often memorize scripture and loved the *Donut Man,* a kid's show with gospel messages. I was very involved in Bible Study Fellowship when she was little, and Karina would go along with me for the kid's group. She drank in the teaching and fully embraced the gospel message of Christ's death on the cross for our sins. One day she was especially touched and wanted to send Jesus a note to tell him how thankful she was that He loved her and had died on the cross for her. I helped her write the note and we attached it to a helium balloon that we released into the air. She clapped with delight at the thought of sending God a thank you note.

During one of the many summers our family spent at Malibu, Ron served a three week assignment as camp manager. Young Karina had the chance to observe the kids and leaders singing, enjoying the silly skits, attending club, and hearing the gospel message clearly explained. In one week's time summer campers at Malibu hear the entire message of the Christian faith. First, they are taught about

God as the creator of all things who desires their friendship. Next, they are told about the problem of sin: how all the self-centered choices we make from the very beginning of life create a vast chasm separating us from Him. In addition, they are told how the grave consequence of these sins is death. The kids have to think about this dilemma for a whole day, wrestling with the question of what can be done about our sin and separation from God. Finally, they are told the good news of how God loved us so much He sent His son, Jesus to pay the price for all we have done wrong. To illustrate, a music video of Michael W. Smith's song "Secret Ambition" was shown to the campers at that time. In graphic detail, it portrays Christ being beaten, bloodied, and nailed to the cross for us. Karina, who was then age three, was in her Daddy's arms as they stood outside the Big Squawka Lodge during club, her little eyes fixed on this video. Even at that young age, she understood that Christ had done this for her. She spontaneously looked up at Ron and said in her sweet little voice, "Oh, Daddy, I love Jesus so much!"

I felt God wanted me, as a parent, to be alert to opportunities to teach our kids about friendship with God through Christ. Thus, I tried to make Him a part of our everyday life. I wanted to keep it real and share how much He loves us and desires our hearts. One day in the car, while we were driving past what used to be a big buffalo farm outside Snohomish, Karina was sitting up front with me. Something in our conversation prompted her to turn and say, "Mom, I want to ask Jesus into my heart." She had been absorbing all of our teaching and that day, it clicked. She was only four, but I knew she was old enough to understand the simplicity of the gospel message. I talked her through an explanation I had learned called ABC:

1. **Admit** that you are a sinner, meaning you have done wrong things, and need Jesus,
2. **Believe** that Jesus was a real person, who died on the cross for you but then came back to life again,
3. **Commit** to being his follower for the rest of your life.

That day in the car, driving past grazing buffalos, she prayed aloud with me to accept Jesus. She knew from then on, Jesus was her Savior and would never let her go. I have never forgotten that moment, nor did she. It was because of this moment of choice, saying "yes" to that little voice inside her four-year old mind, that she could later face the end of her life with confidence and hope. That was her anchoring moment.

Drawing at top opposite page. A sketch from the
book Katie wrote and illustrated for Karina, *Our Special
Treasure*. When Karina was two, she sent a "note" to
Jesus on a helium balloon to thank him for dying on
the cross. She wanted to say how much she loved Jesus.

Photo opposite page. Karina at two and half years old on board
the Malibu Princess on our way to Ron's assignment as
camp manager at Malibu. The family stayed at Malibu
for three weeks.

Sketch by Katie.

Long ago, God had a special plan to make you.

Believe in Jesus...and you will be saved! The disciples were filled with joy! Beloved, let us love one another... Jesus is our strength in trouble... Live in peace with one another!

73

Chapter 8: Karina's Anchored Faith

Accepting Jesus that day in the car, was the beginning of Karina's friendship with Him. She had loved God and believed in Him as a little girl, but now the seed of faith in Christ was firmly planted in her heart. Through Bible study and prayer, it would grow and become the most important aspect of her life. It would shape the things she read, the way she cared about friends, her passion for serving children, and the way she faced her cancer diagnosis. Karina possessed an especially integrated faith for someone so young. While I really do not think it has to be that unique or unusual, at the same time, I do believe the Lord gave her a special sensitivity toward Him.

Since I had found the child's version of *Hind's Feet on High Places* so helpful in my journey, I shared the story with her. I impressed upon her the need for spending personal, special time with Jesus in a secret place, apart from other people and distractions. Just like cultivating a friendship with a new acquaintance, quiet time with the Lord grows our relationship with Him. I told her how prayer is simply talking to God and casting all your cares on Him. I even showed her how it is helpful to write them down in a journal and when she began to read I gave her my first Bible and she was thrilled. She began keeping little prayer journals from a very early age and continued up until the last days of her life. She would pour out her concerns and praises to Him, knowing He heard and cared for her.

Karina's faith was quick to take root and grow, and we nurtured this faith both at home and through Christian school and church. A friend, Shari Monson, and I home schooled Karina and her daughter, Madeline, for the pre-school years. I had the privilege of developing my own curriculum and using my love of teaching to be my own daughter's teacher.

When she was ready for school, we enrolled her in Lighthouse Christian School. Ron's cousin's wife, Deb Robertson, was the kindergarten teacher, and it proved a wonderful learning environment for Karina. Through daily chapel services and Bible teaching, she gained knowledge of scriptures and solidity of faith that is rare to find in adults - let alone kids. Here she learned about the saints of old and first heard about the various missionaries who made huge impacts on our world during the 18th and early 19th centuries. These early days were instrumental in the development of Karina's faith journey.

She had always been the kind of kid who loved books, and as she learned to recognize words, she became an avid reader. There are some people who devour anything written, and she was one. She could walk down the isle of the grocery store, nose buried in a book, oblivious to the world around her. By first grade she had finished the chronicles of Narnia and loved them. She was hungry for information and read everything from novels to missionary stories to political articles. This reading gave her wisdom beyond her years. She was very well-rounded and could converse about a variety of topics.

Of course, in the midst of all of this there was always Young Life. When we moved her to public school in 6th grade, Ron and I became the middle school Young Life coordinators for her school, Kopachuck. As such, we mentored the high school Young Life leaders who helped us and ran the clubs. Those leaders later became our friends and helped us so much during the time of Karina's illness. We were so grateful for their love and support. I was also Karina's Campaigner leader at that time and she and I attended Young Life camp at Break Away Lodge in Oregon. In addition, every summer found us back at Malibu. She absolutely loved the life we had built around camp and Christ and service to others.

While at Lighthouse, Karina had been introduced to various Christian missionaries and developed a keen interest in foreign missions. A number of years earlier I had taken a continuing education course on missions. I would return home from class to find Karina waiting to hear all about it. I passed on to her the information I was learning about various people groups and she, ever curious about different cultures, listened eagerly to my every word. It was the first time I had ever really been exposed to the intricacies of cross-cultural missions and she shared fully in my excitement. When she had a chance to travel to Mexico with a church group, she was quick to sign up and loved the entire experience.

Her interest in foreign missions became the driving force behind her desire to be a missionary in her own neighborhood. We had, by this time, moved into a house down the beach from our first house on Shaw's Cove. It was a lovely waterfront home which Ron had admired many times on his walks along the shore. He desired to live right on the beach, with a dock out front from which he could easily launch a boat. One day he called the owners, Rich and Leanne Seims, and asked if they knew

of anything for sale in the neighborhood like their house on the water. He was
shocked when, during the conversation, they suggested he make an offer on their
house. The very night before they had decided to put their house up for sale as they
felt it had outgrown their needs. Amazingly, they were fellow Christians and the
parents of a son who was on staff with Young Life. Thinking their son could use it
for teen ministry they had developed the property to include a pool, basketball
court, and huge landscaped yard. From the first time we drove onto the property,
Karina felt a deeper calling in the beautiful amenities and beach front. When she
viewed the sprawling grounds, her thought was of its potential to be a mini-Malibu
for young kids in the area. Immediately, she began developing the idea of a kid's
summer camp. She knew exactly how to set it up, for she had been observing the
older kids and adults, such as her own uncle Jim Robertson, running the program
at Malibu for years. The Malibu experience includes funny skits, songs, games,
and activities all geared toward giving kids the best time they have ever
had, and making them laugh so hard they never forget it. Having been
involved with a drama ministry called "His Kids," Karina was very comfortable in
front of an audience. She loved performing and had many creative ideas for
developing the camp curriculum. Therefore, as a mere 6th grader, she became the
program director with her sister and two best friends, Madeline Monson and Aundi
Ragan, enlisted as helpers. Together they developed innovative ideas for making it
a real special week. The summertime backyard Bible camp would be called
"Summer Splash" and her plan was to invite the neighborhood girls for a week of
crafts, games, and all around fun. There was a theme for each day. One day would
be princess day, another spa day, another Olympic day, and the fourth, western
day. The last day would culminate with a talent show where the attendees would
present little skits or dances they had been working on in groups all week. In
between, there was always swimming and crafts. One year there was a carnival
with about six different booths of activities. There was no end to the ideas Karina
came up, with including an egg drop from the top of our deck. In addition, Karina
and her cohorts took turns giving daily talks about Jesus. The underlying goal of
the camp was to share the message of God's love in a creative way through songs,
stories, and dramas. It was so well-organized and made such a big hit that first
summer that she made plans for continuing on the next year. Kids began to look
forward to it every summer and would inevitably say, "This was the best week of my
life!"

Those first young campers still remember this special time and when they see
me today, are eager to express what a fun, creative highlight it was in their
summer. In fact, some of those original campers, Riley and Emerson Price, have

taken over the planning and organizing and, in 2012, in honor of Karina, "Summer Splash" reemerged. Our property once again became host to a whole new generation of young girls. Karina's vision of giving kids a fun week of activity and exposure to the good news of Christ lives on.

Life felt so perfect to me back in those days. As a family we created many happy memories, both at home as well as on our cherished boating adventures. To me, there was no greater joy than being a mom, serving the Lord together with my husband, and raising our three kids to know and love Jesus. Little did I know or predict the storm brewing on the horizon and how it would test our faith. I would need to rely on my anchor like never before.

LIGHTHOUSE CHRISTIAN SCHOOL

by Karina, age 12

**A little piece of my heart
will always be at Lighthouse.**

**Lighthouse Christian School
is more like home.**

Karina wrote these words when she was in
sixth grade in public school, missing her
Christian school. Karina attended Lighthouse
Christian School from kindergarten through fifth
grade. Christian schooling helped anchor her faith.
She loved having faith integrated into all her
subjects, and praying with her teachers and
classmates about everything. She
learned about missionaries who inspired her
for life. She felt she could be herself there.
Karina had a wonderful experience.

a little piece of my heart will always be at Lighthouse.

ANCHOR

LCS is more like home.

HAPPY BIRTHDAY CARD TO KARINA

You will <u>always</u> be our special treasure!
We are <u>so</u> proud of you --- and <u>so</u> blessed to be
your parents! You are the coolest, cutest, most
creative kid --- you are the BEST! We are excited
to see the Lord reveal His plan for you in the
teen years. You really shine! We love you <u>so</u>, <u>so</u> much!
Mom and Dad

Top photo: Karina at her fifties American Girl
doll birthday party when she turned seven.
We served vanilla wafers with chocolate mints in
the middle that looked like little hamburgers and
rootbeer floats. Everyone came in fifties attire with
their doll.

Lower photo: Karina's sixth birthday. She had a
detective party where the kids had to solve a mystery.
Several sixth grade neighborhood girls in detective
overcoats helped by singing and organizing the clues.
Fun was had by all. We always made an effort to make each
birthday special and memorable.
My motto is:
they are only little once.

Sketch by Annika.

Happy Birthday!

you will always be our special treasure! We are so proud of you ~ and so blessed to be your parents! you are the coolest, cutest, creative kid ~ you are the BEST! We are excited to see the Lord reveal His plan for you ~ in the teen years:) You really shine! We love ♥ you so so much!

xoxo ♥ mom + Dad

Photo opposite page: Karina and Annika with their American girl dolls Molly and Kirsten. They loved to play dolls together.

Background opposite page:
The words and drawing are from a page from Annika's book which she made for Karina during the transplant while we were living on our boat on Hunt's Point. Annika was only thirteen when she authored and illustrated a special book for Karina titled *My Sister and Me.* The girls and I often enjoyed drawing and journaling, and creating little books together. Annika's book is about the joy of sisterhood and the activities Karina and Annika shared. Annika and Karina were best friends. Annika's illustrated children's book is available on amazon.com/books. A portion of the profits go to Fred Hutchinson Cancer Research Center in Seattle, WA.

Sketch by Annika.

My Sister and Me was inspired by, well, my sister, Karina, [and] me. Karina was first diagnosed with AMML [ ] June 21, 2005. The rest of that year w[ ] Karina showed great [ ]mission later [ ] in s[ ] for [ ] br[ ] to [ ] t[ ]

a par[ ] Karina is back in goo[ ] [ ]mal life. So naturally, since [ ] relationship with my sister, who [ ]s to be a cancer survivor, I wrote a book showing how close sisters are. They're so close, they've best friends. Just like Karina and I always say: one mind, one marrow. ♡

Robertsons in their dinghy.
Sketches by Katie.

Playing on the beach.

Annika, Erik, and Karina eating berry pie.

Sketches by Katie.

Katie, Karina, and Annika baking their favorite cookies.

Karina and Annika
baking with their
Easy Bake oven.

Karina at Malibu, her favorite place to wakeboard, summer 2004.

Chapter 9: Anchored Amid the Storm

The beginning of the end of my tidy, picturesque life came on June 21st, 2005, Karina's last day of 8th grade, and three days prior to the now annual "Summer Splash" camp. She seemed especially run down, but many of her friends were fighting colds and we attributed it to her recent high level of activity. She had been playing Liesl in the school play *The Sound of Music* and it had been a busy few weeks, both with the musical rehearsals and preparations underway for 8th grade graduation. The last week of school meant a class trip to the Seattle Center and rides at the Fun Forest, then graduation and celebratory outings with girl friends.

We had been to the doctor more than once in recent months. Earlier in the spring, Karina had contracted a bad case of hives. The doctors thought it was just a grass allergy, but the hives persisted and proved a major annoyance to her. Ron and I had plans to go to Malibu for the last weekend of the school year, leaving the kids with babysitters, so I took Karina to the doctor beforehand just to make sure all was well. He agreed with me that she might have a case of mononucleosis, but the test results would not be back for a week. Since she only had a few days left of school, he thought it would be fine for her to finish the year.

We went ahead with our weekend plans but when we returned to find her covered with bruises and begging to skip the last day of school due to fatigue, I knew something must be really wrong. Karina was already somewhat convinced she had leukemia. Thanks to Google, earlier in the spring she had looked up her symptoms online and discovered prolonged hives could be a symptom of leukemia. Of course I found that ridiculous and brushed away her findings. But over the weekend she had again researched her symptoms and reached the same conclusion. Although I did not want to even contemplate that as a diagnosis, I was still very concerned.

On the morning of June 21, the last day of school, my husband had to leave early for a trip to California. I let Karina sleep in late but had scheduled a doctor's appointment. When I took her in he looked her over, took some blood samples, and sent us home. Upon our return, she went to lie on my bed while I went to work out in our fitness area in the garage. I was still hopeful nothing was wrong. Although things did not seem right with her, I reasoned she was simply run down from all the recent activity. I did not fully fathom how bad off she was.

Alarmed with the results of the blood test, the doctor's office immediately called Ron, not knowing he was out of town. He had actually just landed in Southern California when he got the call. The doctor relayed to Ron the results of the blood work and, without delay, he called me with the shocking news - our daughter had leukemia. He told me to take Karina to the hospital as quickly as possible as the doctor wanted her assessed right away. He also advised not worrying her with the diagnosis. Then he turned around and explained his situation to the Alaska Airlines ticketing agent who gave him a seat on a flight back up to Seattle. Once in the air Ron said to himself, *We're gonna beat this. I am smart. I can make things happen.* Ron's business venture was doing very well by now and as I said before, he has a great mind for business and vast entrepreneurial talent. He knew how to stay level headed and make things happen. I, on the other hand, react to the emotion of the moment. Stunned, I almost collapsed, but somehow ran in shock from the garage to the house to the bedroom.

I could not withhold such news from Karina. For one thing, she was a smart girl. She had already made the self-diagnosis. For another, we were very close, and when she saw the look on my face it was confirmation of the bad news. We held each other on the bed and cried. There is no consolation at such a time, only fear and shock. I hurriedly began getting things together to take her to the hospital. Ron had phoned his co-worker's wife to come to the house immediately. As a nurse at Mary Bridge Children's Hospital in Tacoma, she knew exactly who to call to meet us. Thanks to her connections, a nurse, Katie Shields, was already waiting for us when we arrived at the hospital. Katie would quickly become our favorite nurse. She had survived childhood cancer herself and knew how to put us at ease. Her heartfelt care endeared her to us and she quickly won our trust.

As soon as Ron arrived back in the Northwest and joined me at Mary Bridge, we were ushered into the office of pediatric oncologist, Dr. Thomas. Dr. Thomas looked at our information, noticed our address, and concluded we were neighbors. As we discussed this irony, he described to me his Cape Cod style blue house with the red door right up the hill from us. I knew the house instantly as I had run by it for the last ten years, always thinking it was the cutest house on the street, and wondering who lived there. Now, here I was meeting my neighbor, a pediatric oncologist, in a setting I never would have imagined in my wildest dreams. Ironically, he is one of three doctors on staff, but this "just happened" to be his day on duty and we were assigned to him. It turned out to be a huge blessing as he would end up providing house calls at various times throughout our journey due to his close proximity.

He explained the differences between the two kinds of leukemia common in childhood, AML, and ALL, the first more acute and aggressive than the latter, and the various treatment options. AML, while more serious, is more responsive to treatment and therefore, requires less timely and invasive measures. On the other hand, ALL is less serious but must be tackled with a long course of medical intervention. Karina whispered under her breath she hoped for the first. I, of course, hoped for the latter. After blood tests to determine which type she had, they immediately admitted Karina into the hospital where we would camp out for the next two weeks. We would not know which type she had until the labs came back. For now we had to wait and hope.

That first night as we settled into our hospital room, Karina turned to her Bible. In fact, knowing I was sick with anxiety, she reassuringly said, "Mom, don't worry, everything is going to be alright. I just read my verse for the day, Psalm 66:20: 'Praise be to God, who has not rejected my prayer or withheld His love from me!' He is going to take care of me and get us through."

In these brief first hours it had already occurred to Karina she could die from this. But she fixed her hope on the fact that should the worst happen, she would be with her Grammie Jean and with Jesus. She was not afraid. If humankind's greatest fear is death, it just makes sense a loving God would address that by giving his people hope amid that fear. Realizing the gravity of the diagnosis Karina, my 14 year old girl, came face to face with death. But her faith and relationship with Jesus Christ was an anchor, giving her comfort and hope. She was to enter this fight because she wanted to live, but not because she feared death.

We found out the next morning Karina's diagnosis was actually AML, the more acute of the two types of childhood leukemia, but in a form called AMML, which is somewhat less terrible and has a slightly better response to treatment. Grateful does not begin to define my feelings. I was so happy to know we at least had been given a more hopeful diagnosis.

We had to move quickly with treatment, and the next morning, Ron and I were sat down in a room to sign the releases. It was overwhelming. I was in shock at what we were being asked to do and how quickly we were being asked to do it. The plan of action was for five rounds of chemotherapy, and, possibly a bone marrow transplant. We were signing releases to fill our daughter's body with toxic drugs in hopes of saving her life. In a moment of despair my first thought was *we have no pen!* Then I glanced down to see a pen on the floor. It was a small thing, but significant to me: another reminder of how God is in the details.

Overnight our lives were turned upside down. Ron and I alternated between one of us staying with Karina in the hospital while the other would head home to be with the other kids and try to get some sleep. We determined she would never have to be alone and one of us was always at her side from that first diagnosis all the way till the end.

On one of my first nights home, I found myself alone and fearful. I knew getting a good sleep was vital, but I also knew I was distraught, my head hurt and I could use a Tylenol PM. However, I knew there were none in the house. Since friends were asking how they could help, I had put in a request for a box of this medication, but it was getting later and later and no one was coming. I wanted to go to bed and was becoming more and more desperate. I prayed, "Lord please help me!" Immediately that familiar little voice said "Go look in your brief case that is in the linen closet." I did not know why in the world I would look there, of all places, especially since I rarely even use that bag. I did not even know when it had last been used. Nevertheless, I went and found it and peered inside. To my amazement there lay a brand new unopened box of Tylenol PM. The really ironic part was that right after I found it, the doorbell rang and my very thoughtful friend dropped off her box as well. It, however, had expired while mine was fresh. I know that sounds crazy, but I am one of those people who is very aware of expiration dates. If something has expired, I cannot consume it. Once again, I attributed this moment to the Lord's care for me. He meets even my crazy, desperate need to have an unexpired Tylenol PM!

As a runner, I have often been on trail runs where I end up on a stretch of road quite alone. Often I begin to wonder if I have somehow gotten off the route and am lost. Just when I begin to panic, I see the telltale yellow flag marking the path ahead. My journey with Karina's illness was very much like that. Things would go along fine. There would be a lull. Then, all of a sudden, something would happen that left me feeling unsure or even fearful. It was always at those times that God would provide a little yellow sign: a pen on the floor, unexpired Tylenol PM in an obscure place, someone showing up to pray, a random connection, and I would be reassured anew of His love and care. I did not walk this road alone.

When crisis hits one's life everything comes to a screeching halt in the struggle to survive. All else seems trivial. Karina's cancer was not the first crisis for me but it was certainly the most frightening. I felt like I was on a tiny boat in the midst of a huge storm. In fact, it seemed as if we could easily drown beneath the overwhelming waves. Again the scripture spoke hope into my heart. Jesus' disciples had encountered a similar situation. In the midst of a very real storm they cried out to Him;

"'Master, master, we are going to drown'. He got up, rebuked the wind and the raging waters; the storm subsided, and all was calm..."
(Luke 8:24).

We were in the midst of a crisis but I knew for certain we were not alone and He would get our family through whatever lay ahead. Like the massive anchor on *Epiphany*, my hope in the love of Christ would hold me in this storm.

During that first round of treatment a couple stopped by to pray. While in prayer, they had a very specific vision of God's love being like a magnet drawing us into Him, and they shared this with me. Shortly thereafter, Karina developed an infection and had to be taken down to the basement of the hospital for a CAT scan. This area felt cold, lonely and far-removed from anything living and vibrant. As we approached the CAT scan entrance, the doors caught my eye. They were painted like a huge magnet with red tips. Bold words overhead proclaimed: "POWER ALWAYS ON." I recalled the vision and smiled as I realized this "yellow marker" from the Lord. His love is a magnet drawing us into Him. He will never leave us even in our darkest, "basement" hours.

Another procedure we encountered in the first round of treatment was testing to see if either Ron or I were a compatible match to serve as a donor of platelets for Karina. At first, she was given regular donor platelets, but she developed a nose bleed that could not be stopped. This alerted them to her need for a better match. I hate needles and was scared to death of this procedure and what might be required of me. But to my great relief, Ron went first and turned out to be a perfect match. During Karina's illness, my husband would earn the hospital's record for donating the most platelets. Whenever she was in need, they would call on him to donate. He would do so as frequently as needed, sometimes every two to three days so that Karina would have the necessary platelets. Quietly and selflessly he would go to the hospital and make his donation: his life for hers. Ron was the ever-loving father, willing to give his all to save his dying child.

I know many people are confused by Christianity, but this service Ron provided our daughter is the simplest example I have for explaining the gospel. God, our loving father, seeing that we, His children, were dying from an incurable disease (sin), gave us His own blood so that we could be saved. This, in a nutshell, is a picture of the love of God.

Four days into the initial diagnosis, I was exhausted. So much had happened so fast. I felt sick with worry. It was June 24, and I realized I had failed to read from a daily devotional the day before. I had been enjoying a classic book by Oswald Chambers, but today I was just too tired. I intended to skip over the missed reading when the book fell open to that very entry, as if it should not be missed:

June 23: *"This sickness will not be unto death, but will be to bring glory to my Father in heaven."* John 11:3

I knew these were words Jesus had spoken to his friends, Mary and Martha, when their brother Lazarus had died. All three were believers in Jesus, in His healing power, and in His promise of life after death. When Jesus spoke these words, the grieving sisters assumed He referred to spiritual healing and thought He was reassuring them their brother was in heaven. But Jesus was referring to a physical healing and went on to literally call Lazarus back to life from the grave. Their brother was given physical life and lived a number more years before his final death. I reread the page carefully as the promising words jumped out at me. Could it be the Lord was giving me hope and reassurance that Karina's illness would not end in death? I knew she would be given eternal life if she died, but was He promising to extend her worldly life? I believed He was, and I held to this promise firmly and confidently throughout every part of our dark journey.

Karina was in the hospital twelve days for that first round of chemotherapy treatment. From the beginning she was a most gracious patient, always thanking the nurses and doctors for every procedure they did, however painful. This attitude would continue through every medical intervention and hospital stay she endured over the next few years. Even at the very end of her life, she thanked the nurses and aides and was a kind, uncomplaining patient.

She lost all of her hair within that time, and of course, being 14, this was a big deal to her. She felt her hair loss had left her unattractive. Worried about how this would affect future romantic prospects she asked me, "Mom, do you think anyone will ever like me or take me to a dance?"

I reassured her that, of course, they would, but truthfully, I wondered myself if it would happen. At this point, I did not think Karina would die, but there was something in me that questioned how my daughter would be treated now that she had cancer. I did not need to fear for her friends loved her through it all, and later we would experience the joy of watching a boy she really liked escort her to many dances. He showed he cared about her as a person through every wig and hair style she would have.

As the fourth of July approached, we begged to go home. Dr. Thomas signed the release knowing he could easily make a house call if needed. It felt so good to bring Karina back to our seaside home for the holiday. In the two weeks since we had been gone, Mari Misterek, one of my best friends, had completely redone Karina's room. Prior to that, Karina had slept on the top bunk of beds we had for the girls, but we knew in her weak state she would never be able to climb up the ladder. Mari lovingly brought in a new bed and painted and arranged the room to be perfect for her. Friends like this provided such a service to us during those difficult days. We are forever grateful for such an outpouring of love and care.

Dr. Thomas checked in with us that first day and kept close tabs the next as well. But we had barely been home when we were forced to return to the hospital. Karina had developed an intestinal infection, which is a common side effect of chemotherapy. Although it made her very ill, it also served as a mixed blessing as it led the doctors to discover a pre-existing condition which had been making her sick periodically her whole life. Once or twice a year since birth, she would develop a bad side ache, and we never knew why. A scan revealed she had an obstructed kidney. This led to kidney surgery later in July to correct the condition. Although she was left extremely weak, all went well she began to feel better.

By August things were going fairly smoothly. We bought her a wig, and although she was not completely done with treatments we eventually got to go out on *Epiphany*. We had been so looking forward to our first summer spent on the boat. By late in the season she was free from infections and released to finally go with us. We were thrilled. Though she was weak and tired, she never complained, and indeed the sea air revitalized her and us. It felt wonderfully normal to be back on the water visiting all of our favorite ports: a blessed reprieve from the last few dreadful months.

Top photo, opposite page: Karina with friends Madeline Monson and Aundi Ragan in the middle school musical *The Sound of Music*. Karina had one of the lead roles as Liesl. Karina loved drama and one of her favorite movies was The Sound of Music.

Lower photo, opposite page: Karina and her best friends Madeline and Aundi. In sixth grade, Karina started a day camp for girls called Summer Splash. She wanted to start a mini Malibu because she loved going to camp herself. She invited thirty to fifty girls ages kindergarten to fifth grade for a week of fun activity. Karina and her friends were the program directors. Katie was the camp manager. Annika and her friends were the young counselors who supervised the smaller groups of girls. The week consisted of daily themes including Princess Day, Spa Day, Olympics, Carnival Day, and many more. The girls swam, sang, and learned arts and crafts. Each group made an act for a talent show at the end of the week. At the end of each day, Karina or one of her friends would give a message about Jesus to the girls. Karina ran Summer Splash for three summers, and Katie and Annika continue to run the camp (with former campers as the program directors) in memory of Karina.

Best Buds!

THE SOUND OF MUSIC

Friends

Photo opposite page: Karina, Annika, and Erik.
A happy spring break in 2005.

JUNE 23 DEVOTION
FROM <u>DEVOTIONS FOR A DEEPER LIFE</u>

Suggested reading: John 11:1-17
When Jesus heard that, he said, This sickness is not
unto death, but for the glory of God, that the Son of
God might be glorified thereby (that is John 11:4).

This verse gave me hope and strengthened me for our
journey.

Sketch by Katie.

Glory to God in the Highest

Anthem for Mixed Voices, A Cappella
(S. A. T. B.)

Luke 2:14   HOMER WHITFORD

The message of the angels is here set anew in simple contrapuntal style. There is a steady interweaving of the imitative motives and a constant building up of volume to a full close, resulting in a most effective anthem.—

SUGGESTED READING: JOHN 11:1–17

When Jesus heard that, he said, This sickness is not unto death, but for the glory of God, that the Son of God might be glorified thereby. (John 11:4).

The New Testament mentions quite a few sick souls. Take Thomas for example.

Why do I mention Thomas? Because he was very loyal to Jesus Christ, but he was very gloomy. He took the sick view of life. He always thought the worst was going to happen—and the worst always did happen! There was no use going to Thomas and saying, "Cheer up." He knew you could not alter facts by saying that.

Every time you hear from Thomas, he says something about death or disease. When Lazarus died, and Jesus said He was going to the place where Lazarus was buried, Thomas said, "Let us also go, that we may die with Him."

JUNE 23

117

KARINA'S SCRAPBOOK PAGE

Upper left photo. Karina's school picture from freshman year. Karina is wearing her wig.

Upper right photo. Karina's eighth grade graduation, the day before she was diagnosed.

Middle photo. Karina right after she lost her hair, the first diagnosis.

Lower left photo. One of the first days in the hospital. Karina comforted me after reading **Psalm 66:19-20**

   ...but God has surely listened and heard my voice in prayer, praise be to God, who has not rejected my prayer or withheld His love from me!

She assured me that, "Mom, everything will be alright."

Lower right photo. Karina and Annika in the summer, between treatments.

My eighth grade graduation, the day before I was diagnosed

My school picture freshman year

One of the first days in the hospital

Annika and I in the summer, between treatments

Chapter 10: Anchored Amid Fear

September arrived and Karina entered her freshman year of high school. We celebrated her 15th birthday on the boat, and I found myself thinking, *We can do this. It's not that bad. We just do a treatment and then pray to avoid infection. We can handle it.*

Just when we settled into a routine, fever hit at the end of the month, and we had to go back into the hospital. Karina had developed an infection which then turned into pneumonia.

It grew increasingly severe until she couldn't breathe on her own. While she was taken to the ICU, Ron and I were taken to a back room and shown slides of her lungs. It was serious, and the doctor gave no false hope. He asked us how we would want her to die and laid out the options. Later, sitting next to Karina's bed, I cried out, "Lord! Show us you're HERE!" I was nearly shouting aloud. Inside I was crying out, *Lord what about the verse? 'This sickness shall not end in death?' What about your promise?*

Immediately He showed up through the presence of two sets of people. First, I turned to see four guys we knew from church. They had no idea Karina had been transferred to the ICU, but while praying together that morning had felt led to come down to the hospital right away to encourage us. They took Ron to a quiet room and prayed for him. Next, they took me aside, but I was clearly in a state of confusion. I told them of the reassurance I had received from the Lord earlier in the summer and of my despair at this turn of events. I told them I was convinced the promise "this sickness shall not end in death" had been given me. They calmly and powerfully prayed for me. At times like this our minds can be filled with fear and doubt but the Lord has promised peace and confidence especially when we come to Him in prayer. Their prayer helped remind me of this, and I felt immediate peace.

The second person to "show up" was Adam, a traveling nurse from Boston. He had been with us since the beginning of the diagnosis and had experience with pediatric cancer patients. He was off duty, but felt prompted to come by and check on us. He was wearing street clothes as he walked into our room. When he heard the situation, he relayed to us how often this happens and that it does not always mean it's the end. Often it is just a setback. His reassurance gave me hope. Soon after the prayer and Adam's visit, Karina started getting better. In fact, that night she improved to the point where the doctor told Ron to go ahead and leave for our son's football game. We took that as very good news.

Hope is so important when we are in the dark places. Over and over in the Bible, we are told to hope. We are not to live in despair. No matter the outcome, we are to place our hope in the love God has for us and the promise He will be with us and give us a future. We can be confidently optimistic as we face trials. We were especially blessed by the medical professionals who spoke hope to us when we were walking in the valley of the shadow of death. Even if it is just a glimmer, hope is the nourishment the soul needs when facing bleak and dismal hardships.

We stayed in the hospital for six weeks waiting for Karina's blood counts to return to a healthy level. Every day her blood was tested and every day we awaited the results. All the while my husband kept donating his healthy platelets. Our complete focus was on bringing her back to health. Finally, by the sixth week, much to my relief and in answer to our many desperate prayers, the counts started to come up. It had been a very bleak situation for she lacked the white blood cells in which to fight off the pneumonia, and we were well aware we had almost lost her. The protocol from the beginning was for five rounds of chemotherapy, but her body was too weak from the pneumonia to finish the fifth round. I was always haunted by this and wondered in the back of my mind if she would be okay with only four. But for now I was grateful for the miracle we had been given.

It was mid-November when we were given the clearance to bring her home. While she could not return to school until February she was able to go on a family trip to Hawaii in January. Then we were blessed with a "Make a Wish" Disney cruise in April. During the time in the ICU she would talk somewhat in her sleep about being in the water. We knew she was referring to swimming and wake boarding which she especially loved to do at Malibu. Karina absolutely loved being in the water and watching her swim with the dolphins and snorkel in the Bahamas during the cruise felt very good indeed. She was once again enjoying health and we, her happy parents, were thrilled with seeing her alive!

Photo above right: Karina's fifteenth birthday, in 2005, just after her third round of chemotherapy. She enjoyed time with her best friends on Epiphany on a trip to Seattle for shopping, dinner, and fun.

Opposite page, Katie's prayer journal entry:
Lord, my little girl is so precious --- I just can't stand
that she has this disease --- please remove it from her.

Bottom photo opposite page: Karina, Annika, and Katie on a summer boating trip at Roche Harbor in 2005. Shortly after diagnosis, Karina is sporting her ponytail wig. We enjoyed family time on our boat, and took little adventures in our dinghy during the day.   The kids enjoyed looking at the maps and choosing where we would explore the next day. Doing things a normal way gave us great joy and we loved being away from the hospital in the fresh salt air and being together.

Sketch by Katie.

Lord, my little girl is so precious — I just can't stand that she has this disease. Please remove it from her —

FROM KARINA'S PRAYER JOURNAL

Written around her sixteenth birthday, the year after she was diagnosed the first time.

Dear Lord,
I am so worried and nervous about driver's ed. I have to get my drives done, but it's so hard and nerve wracking. I need to remember Phil. 4:13:

> *I can do everything through Christ who gives me strength.*

but its so difficult --- help me to rely on You for strength.

Thanks for this great summer --- it's so much better than last year. And thanks for the miracle of Kelsey. I <u>love</u> that kid so much! Please bless her and her family in everything she does.

Photo: Karina and her cousin Kelsey. Kelsey was an answer to prayers for Karina's Uncle Jim and Aunt Michelle. She is truly a blessing.

I'm so worried/nervous about driver's ed. I have to get my drives done, but its so hard and nerveracking. I need to remember Phil. 4:13, but its so difficult—help me to rely on you for strength.

Thanks for this great summer—it's so much better than last year. And thanks for the miracle of Kelsey, I love that kid so much!!! Please bless her & her family in everything she does.

Chapter 11: One Mind, One Marrow

The summer of 2006 went really well. We had made it through the first year and past the anniversary of Karina's diagnosis. We were filled with gratitude at how the Lord had preserved her life and given us strength when we needed it. *Epiphany* served as our ready retreat, and we went out on her as often as we could. Except for Karina's check-ups, life again took on a sweet and welcome normality. Our regular doctor's visits were always the same: a blood draw followed by waiting to hear how the cell counts looked. With bated breath we always hoped for the same outcome: the doctor walking out of his office with a smile and thumbs up saying, "Things look great."

September came around and the kids started back to school. Ron and I had been invited to accompany some friends who were looking to buy a yacht at the Monaco boat show. We loved attending the various shows when we could, and this one was especially exciting. It was to be my first time traveling overseas, but I was struggling with the trip. The kids did not want us to go, and I really did not feel excited about leaving. Karina's sophomore year had just started, and she was feeling good again, enjoying friends, school, and being on the swim team. I had no explanation for the unsettled feeling in my gut, so we continued with our plans.

When we got home, even though an appointment was not scheduled until October, I took Karina to the doctor straight away. I had an uneasy feeling after seeing a bruise on her shin. She justified it as being from getting into the pool, and maybe it was a mother's intuition, but I just wanted to have her checked out. Karina did not agree as seen from her journal:

9/25/06

Just because I have a little sore throat & a couple bruises they think its back!!!!! It's not!!!!! I know it isn't!!!!!!!Why can't they have some faith and trust? I'M OKAY!!!! I don't even want to be around them right now—they can't treat me like a normal person!!

The blood work revealed the worst of my fears. The cancer was back, and Karina needed to start chemotherapy without delay. This time, the doctor decided to move ahead with a bone marrow transplant. When Karina had first been diagnosed a year earlier, we had been sent to the Fred Hutchinson Cancer Research Center, or the Fred Hutch, as it is called in the Northwest, for a consult. Well known as a world famous cancer treatment center, it is here that Dr. Donnall Thomas, creator of bone marrow transplantation, won a Nobel Prize for his pioneering work in the field. When others said it could never be done, he believed in the use of bone marrow transplants as a method for treating cancer and proved it was an effective intervention with a high success rate. A year earlier, we had each been tested to see if anyone was a match for a bone marrow transplant should it ever be needed. Only 30 percent of siblings have a match on bone marrow, but much to our surprise, our girls were an identical match. Our daughter Annika would be a donor if it ever came to that, which we prayed it would not. As successful as it is, it is also quite an invasive procedure and we were relieved when it was decided, a year earlier, that Karina would not need it. Now however, things had changed and it became the recommended treatment. We needed to get the ball rolling in this direction with Annika as the donor. Given its reputation in the field, we knew we would be in very good hands at the Fred Hutch. However we would be required to live within 15 minutes of the center for 100 days.

Knowing we had a treatment plan in place was of great comfort to me. Karina would return to the hospital in Tacoma for chemotherapy in hopes of getting her into remission for the upcoming transplant, which would occur in Seattle. After just one round of chemotherapy, Karina was in remission and it was determined she would be able to handle the transplant. Thus we made plans to move, temporarily, to Seattle, Washington.

As we prepared to leave our house in Gig Harbor, I felt weary. Karina was sick once again and needed more medical intervention, but this time we would be displaced from the home we love and the familiar supportive community around us. How could I make it through another time? We had dealt with cancer once, and the thought of going through it again was beyond overwhelming. I felt defeated and scared to death. My twin sister, Sara, an avid runner like me, comforted me by saying, "Don't worry Kate it's just like a race course. The second time through is faster and smoother than the first.

You'll get through it." Buoyed by this encouragement, and renewed in hope, I set my mind toward finding our new home.

It was required we live not only within 15 minutes of the Fred Hutch but also Seattle Children's Hospital. We had a couple ideas for a place, but they seemed to be falling through. Living on *Epiphany* arose as the most viable option; however moorage was proving a dilemma. Lake Union is in the middle of the city and right across the street from the Fred Hutch, but knowing our two younger children would be left alone a lot, I was uneasy of the city surroundings. As it turned out, some good friends, the Radandts, had just bought the property of former hydroplane racer Stan Sayers on Lake Washington. Located at the end of Hunt's Point in Bellevue, the property was in a private and well patrolled neighborhood close to the hospitals yet outside the downtown corridor. Less than a year prior we had been out to see this property and had loved the beauty of the area. In fact, at that time I had said, "Oh, I could live on this road!" Now those words were to become a self-fulfilling prophesy.

Epiphany is a big boat and needs a sturdy dock, which is not so easily found, so one day Ron went to check out the structure on the Radandt's property. While there he bumped into an acquaintance, Lane Sapp, whom we had met the previous Memorial Day on our first *Epiphany* trip to Roche Harbor. Back then, Ron, in his friendly way, had struck up a conversation with this fellow boater. One thing led to another, and soon we were dining on Lane's yacht like old friends. Randomly seeing this boating friend out of the blue on the very day Ron was investigating the use of the Hunt's Point property was an amazing irony, or as we would say, amazing providence.

Lane also lives on Hunt's Point and was renovating a house and lengthening his dock. That very day, the contractors were there doing the work. Ron explained the need for a place to moor our boat while Karina was in treatment. He also explained the difficulty of the existing dock on our friends' property not being strong enough. Hearing the dilemma, Lane immediately offered his contractors to come and strengthen the structure so that it would accommodate our 68' *Epiphany*. Within 24 hours we had safe and adequate moorage for our new home, exactly 15 minutes from both the treatment center and the hospital. We could not believe how perfectly suited and beautiful this place was for us. We were in awe of God's provision.

Epiphany had now become our ark, a place of safety in the midst of our storm.

Right smack in the middle of this surreal and awful trial for our family, God gave us a lovely, serene place to live. Over the next few months we got to know many neighbors in the area, and a dream formed of hosting a future couple's weekend at Malibu where we could share our favorite place as well as our faith. In addition, I was at ease knowing Erik and Annika were safe whenever we had to be away at the hospital attending to Karina. We felt so fortunate and grateful for God's incredible provision.

During one of the nights on the boat waiting the day of the transplant, I could not sleep. Restless, I picked up my Bible for solace. It fell open to Luke 8 and the red letters highlighting Jesus' own words jumped off the page: "Don't be afraid, just believe, and she will be healed." Once again, I was amazed at how words spoken 2,000 years ago offered me hope in my present circumstances. As I read further, I discovered a parent like myself, sick with grief over the thought of losing his little girl. Although he was a Jewish leader, he had heard of the healing power of Christ and, like me, came pleading for the life of his daughter. Many people would themselves rather die than approach Jesus, but parents of dying children are desperate. In humility he overcame the rigid rules of religion and simply came to Christ with his need. Jesus immediately followed the man through the crowd to his house. On the way, however, the Jewish man received the devastating news that it was too late and the girl had already died. But Jesus was unhindered. Ignoring the report, he comforted the man, "Don't be afraid, just believe and she will be healed." Then, Jesus continued on to the house where he proceeded to raise the girl from her deathbed to the astonishment of the mourners present. That night Jesus spoke those same words of comfort and hope into my heart, and I was deeply reassured.

The first week of treatment was completed at the Fred Hutch outpatient center where Karina was given drugs to kill off her bone marrow. We were thankful she could complete this procedure as an outpatient rather than be admitted to the hospital but were warned taking care of her on the boat would be difficult. Ron and I had to learn how to clean her central line and administer the IV drugs on our own. Annika was a big help, as we all had to pitch in and play the role of nurse. Cleaning wounds and giving shots are not tasks in which I am gifted, but I knew I would do anything to help my daughter. By the end of the week we were all weary, and she was so sick and frail we knew we could no longer care for her on the boat. Sadly, we had to admit her to Children's hospital.

In the meantime Annika was scheduled for an appointment at the Fred Hutch to receive booster shots to increase her stem cells. On November 20, when it came time for the procedure, our brave younger daughter at just 13 years old donated all the needed cells within just four hours. The staff was amazed as this process generally takes much longer. As she donated her blood, it was processed through a machine that separated her stem cells into a big bag. That bag would then be brought to Karina who was across town in Children's hospital. There, in the highly sterile environment of the bone marrow unit, Karina, who was by now completely void of her own marrow, would receive Annika's life giving stem cells as a replacement.

November 21 was the actual transplant day. The nurses treated it like a second birthday with balloons and celebratory posters to mark the event. Karina received the bag of Annika's marrow intravenously in a process that took about two hours. She made it look so easy. It was unbelievable to think how a simple bag of fluid stem cells transported from the Fred Hutch to Children's in a little red cooler could give a person a new lease on life. Ultimately this medical miracle would give Karina three more perfect years. Not knowing that at the time, all we could do was watch, wait, and hope, that Annika's stem cells would breathe renewed life into Karina's body.

After the transplant we were required to stay in the area for 100 days. Our time was spent in the comforting surrounds of *Epiphany*, which was moored ironically in a place called Cozy Cove, where we homeschooled the kids and enjoyed a great time of family bonding. We were especially touched by the generosity of the Hunt's point community. We had to spend Christmas there but found ourselves well cared for by neighbors who kindly provided us with a ham dinner. Many others brought meals, invited us into their homes, and made us feel loved with their many acts of kindness. Everyone was so welcoming and generous. The Radandts even orchestrated our use of the Bellevue club, which was a huge blessing to our family. To have a place to work out and swim was so fun and relaxing during that long winter. We had nothing else to do during this time except be together and take care of Karina. She needed regular check-ups to make sure things were still going well, and much to our relief it was. She experienced no complications of any kind and the doctor even gave her a "gold star." Slowly her numbers started coming up. She had received the stem cells from Annika with no problem, as her body proved to be a perfect host.

Due to Karina's frail immunity, we could not go anywhere there were lots of people. No trips out to the mall or to restaurants, and people could only come to visit if they were absolutely healthy. We also became keenly aware of the germs around us, or rather, keeping them away from Karina. Purell became our best friend as we obsessed over keeping a clean and germ-free environment.

Toward the end of the 100 days, we could take Karina out to public places if we avoided big crowds, and we began enjoying some normal outings once again. Right at the top of the dock was a huge garage left over from a Stan Sayer's hydroplane. It proved to be another small but serious blessing. We were able to use it for our car, which was perfect as it was so close, and Karina, who remained very weak and frail, did not have to walk far when we went out. Today we have a piece of that demolished garage as our mantle in our outdoor fireplace. It serves as yet another reminder of the many little ways the Lord cared for us during that difficult time.

The required stay in Seattle came to a close, and we returned home to our Gig Harbor house on March 4, 2007. What we had thought would be a terrible time turned out to be one of blessing and bonding for our family as well as a great experience with the nurturing community of Hunt's Point. We are so thankful for the friendships begun in adversity that continue today.

While we were away we had remodeled an area of our home to accommodate a new bedroom so the girls would no longer need to share, but they continued to stay in one room. They had always been extremely close as sisters and friends, and now that Annika had shared her stem cells, they were bonded in an even deeper way. During the time on the boat, she wrote and illustrated an adorable and touching book for Karina called *My Sister and Me*. It perfectly detailed their deep affection for one another. Now, having shared this unique experience, and DNA, their new motto became: "one mind, one marrow."

KARINA'S PRAYER JOURNAL
October 16, 2006
BEFORE WE LEFT HOME FOR THE TRANSPLANT

Joshua 1:9
Don't worry or be scared. Even in the <u>really</u> hard times.

Joshua 1:15
First, have to do something difficult, then rest after.
---sick now (that's the battle), then better (that's the rest).

1:16 *Life Application Bible.* "If we are going to complete
the tasks God has given us, we must fully agree to his
plan, pledge ourselves to obey it, and put his principle into
action." (Just like the Israelites had to agree with leader's
plan before carrying it out).

I sometimes don't agree with God's plan --- like getting
sick again. I need to remember He knows what's best and
has the best plan.

10/16/06

Joshua 1:9 - don't worry or be scared b/c God will always be w/ you, even in the really hard times.

1:15 - first have to do something difficult, then rest after...
- sick now (battle), then better (rest

1:16 - Life Application - "If we are going to complete the tasks God has given us, we must fully agree to his plan, pledge ourselves to obey it, and put his principle into action" (Just like Iraelites had to agree w/ leader's plan before carrying it out.)
- I sometimes don't agree w/ God's plan - like getting sick again, I need to remember he knows what's best and has the best plan

115

KARINA'S PRAYER JOURNAL
October 29, 2006
AT HOME BEFORE LEAVING FOR
THE TRANSPLANT

Joshua 24
23, Life Application talked about how we should throw
away the idols in our lives, just as the Israelites did. The
idols aren't literal (they could be though), they are the sin
and things that distract us from following God with our
whole heart. We need to get rid of them.

Joshua did some amazing things with God as his leader.
He trusted God with everything. He won all his battles,
because he trusted God's plan and didn't doubt it. This is
something I need to work on. Please help me.

KARINA'S PRAYER JOURNAL
October 31, 2006

Psalm 77 talks about going through hard times, and
remembering how all the other times, God has come through
for us. Doing that helps us remember that God helped us
then and he will help us again. It should also strengthen
our faith and trust in God because we know from experience
he will help us.

Joshua 24

23, Life Application talked about how we should through away the idols in our lives, just as the Israelites did. The idols aren't literal (they could be though) they're the sin and things that distract us from following God with our whole heart. We need to get rid of them.

* Joshua did some amazing things with God as his leader. He trusted God with everything. He won all his battles because he trusted God's plan and didn't doubt it. This is something I need to work on. Please help me

Psalm 77 talks about going through hard times, and how remembering all the other times God has come through for us. Doing that helps us remember that God helped us then, and he'll help us again. It should also strengthen our faith & trust in God b/c we know from experience He will help us.

Karina prays to the Lord:

Transplant is the day after tomorrow, that's when life begins again. I dunno, it's kinda weird me and Annika are gonna have the same bone marrow/immune. I totally wouldn't want anyone else's. One effect of the whole thing is that I probably won't be able to have kids. That makes me sad, knowing that the chances of my future husband and I having a child are slim. Doctor said some people have been able to, miraculously. Please, let me have one baby that is my own. I don't know how I feel about everything. Sometimes I'm really mad, and blame You and ask why. But I remember You have a plan for me, and something good will come out of it. Just let the next year go by fast.

      Love,
         Karina

11/19/00

Transplant is the day after tomorrow, that's when life begins again. I dunno, it's kinda weird me + Annika are gonna have the same bone marrow immune. I totally wouldn't want anyone else's. One effect of the whole thing is that I probaly won't be able to have kids. That makes me sad knowing that the chances of my future husband and I having a child are slim. Dr. said some people have been able too, miracously. Please let me have one baby that's my own.

I don't know how I feel about everything. Sometimes I'm really mad and blame you and ask why, but I remember you have a plan for me, and something

119

KATIE'S PRAYER JOURNAL
A FEW DAYS BEFORE THE TRANSPLANT
November 19, 2006

Lord,

I come to you in faith asking you to heal my (our) daughter completely here on this earth. I know she belongs to you and that we are in Your hands --- she is yours. I really believe that. Oh Lord, thank you for her! We ask for a miracle, that You would move this mountain from us, that Karina would be able to enjoy a long life here on earth! Lord, thank you so much for her --- she is so special and precious to me! Please give me assurance, Lord, that she will be okay --- that you are with us! We want to share you with others and tell of your wonders and what you are and will be doing for our family.

The Lord's right hand has done mighty things!

I will **NOT** die but live and proclaim what the Lord has done!

I will give thanks because you have answered me!

Nov. 19, 2006

Lord, I come to you in faith
asking you to heal my
(our) daughter completely – I
here on this earth – I
know she belongs to you
and that we are in your
hands – she is yours.
I really believe that –
Oh Lord thankyou for her!
We ask for a miracle that
you would move this
mountain from us – that
Karina would be able to
enjoy a long life here on
earth! Lord thankyou so
much for her – she is
so special and precious
to me! Please give me
assurance Lord that she
will be ok – that you are
with us! We want to share
you w/ others – and tell
of your wonders – and what
you are + will be doing
for our family –

the Lord's right hand
has done mighty things!

I will NOT die but
live + proclaim what
the Lord has done!

I will give thanks
because you have answered
me

121

TRANSPLANT DAY
NOVEMBER 21, 2006
KARINA'S NEW BIRTHDAY

Top photo: Thirteen year old Annika donating her stem cells.   The procedure took four hours. The needles were huge! She did a great job.

Middle photo: The bag of Annika's stem cells which would give Karina new life.

Lower photo: Poster the nurses made to celebrate transplant day. We had a huge celebration that day with the nurses, the doctors, and our family.

SEATTLE
CANCER CARE
ALLIANCE

My sister donating her stem cells

I can do everything through him who gives me strength. _Philippians 4:13_

My new stem cells

...RED
...UTCHINSON
...ANCER
...ESEARCH
...ENTER

...bert W. Day
...mpus

Happy
Transplant
Day!!

Poster the nurses made

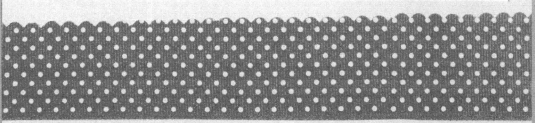

KATIE'S PRAYER JOURNAL
THE DAY AFTER TRANSPLANT
IN THE HOSPITAL
November 22, 2006

Lord,

Thank you for Karina's new start today --- yesterday
was big --- NOV 21 transplant day!! New blood ---
stem cells from Annika --- I am truly amazed! Lord,
you know my thoughts, my insecurities --- I still can't
believe the perfect match our girls are...Thank you that
you made them that way. I love you and don't know
what I would do without you! Bless Karina and Ron
today. Lord I ask that you remove --- prevent any
severe side effects/problems that can occur. You know
YOU are all knowing. She is yours. Take care of her.
Give us wisdom on what she needs...

I ask that you would allow a miracle for her. We believe
in your power at work in us --- please heal her from this
disease. Use us, shine through us.

Nov. 22nd

Lord,
thankyou for Karina's new
start today - Yesterday was
big "New blood - stemcells
day." NOV 21st transplant
from Annika - I am truly
amazed! Lord, you know my
thoughts, my insecurities ...
I still can't believe the perfect
match our girls are...
thankyou that you made
them that way Lord I love
you and don't know what
I would do w/out you!
Bless Karina + Ron today
Lord I ask that you remove -
prevent any severe side effects/
problems that can occur - you
know - you are all knowing
she's yours - take care of
her - give us wisdom on what
she needs Lord ...

I ask that you would allow
a miracle for her! We believe
in your power at work in us -
please heal her from this
disease! Use us, shine ⭐
thru us

125

KARINA'S PRAYER JOURNAL
DURING THE 100 DAYS AFTER TRANSPLANT
February 15, 2007

My Utmost For His Highest (a favorite devotional book of Karina's by Oswald Chambers) **for today, reminds me of Hadassah from my books. She suffered and served so that others might come to Christ.**

Love,

Karina

A year later, when I was going through Karina's entries, I came upon this entry and wondered who Hadassah was. I realized she was the main character in a series of books Karina loved, the *"Mark of the Lion"* series by Francine Rivers. I found her books in her bookcase and read. I couldn't put them down. Hadassah inspired me, too. I could see Karina in her. The books are historical fiction set in Biblical times. I would recommend them to anyone.

Jeremiah 29:11
For I know the plans I have for you, declares the Lord, plans to prosper you and not to harm you, plans to give you hope and a future.

This verse is one of Karina's favorites. She memorized it when she was a little girl.

2/15/07

<u>My utmost For His Highest</u> for today reminds me of Hadassah from my books. She suffered and served so that others might come to Christ.

Love,
Karina

Jeremiah 29:11 For I know the plans I have for you, declares the Lord, plans to prosper you and not to harm you, plans to give you hope and a future.

Love,
Karina

KARINA'S PRAYER JOURNAL DURING HER
100 DAYS OF ISOLATION
WITH US AFTER THE TRANSPLANT
February 16, 2007

Lord,

Thanks that everything is going so well!!! Yet again, You came through for me. Why do I ever doubt? I know you are going to take care of me. You have shown me before I <u>always</u> need to trust You, no matter what. Please let things continue to go well with me --- please don't let me get any GVHD (graft versus host disease)!!!

(A note to herself) **Look up in Life Application** (a supplement to her study Bible).

1 John 1: 5-7

This is the message we have heard from him and declare to you: God is light; in him there is no darkness at all. If we claim to have fellowship with him, yet walk in the darkness, we lie and do not live by the truth. But, if we walk in the light, as he is in the light, we have fellowship with one another, and the blood of Jesus, his Son, purifies us from all sin.

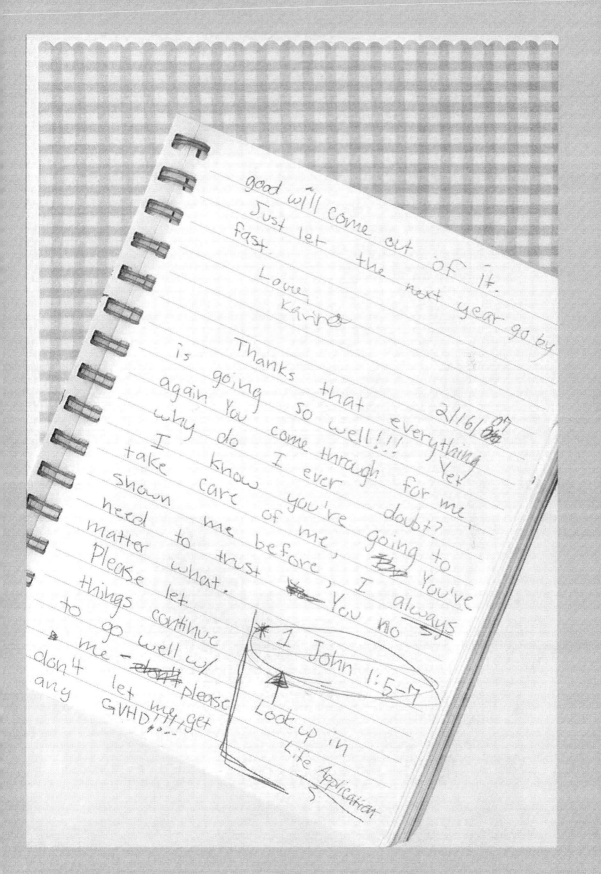

good will come out of it. Just let the next year go by fast.

Love,
Karine

2/16/07

Thanks that everything is going so well!!! Yet again You come through for me. Why do I ever doubt? I know you're going to take care of me, By You've shown me before, I always need to trust You no matter what. You Please let things continue to go well w/ me — ~~don't~~ please don't let me get any GVHD!!!...

*1 John 1:5-7

Look up in Life Application

129

KARINA'S PRAYER JOURNAL
MARCH 3, 2007
THE LAST DAY BEFORE RETURNING HOME
AFTER THE 100 DAY TRANSPLANT STAY

Karina prays to the Lord:

I can't believe we go home tomorrow!!! I've been packing, geez, I have accumulated a <u>ton</u> of crap. It's taking me forever to figure out where to put things. I am taking a break right now, I just filled up my whole bag, its gonna be heavy. The last three months have flown by, I feel like I blinked, and it was over, which I'm glad of. It will be really nice to be back home in Gig Harbor and start to get in the swing of things. I'm so thankful everything is going well. I really hope the chronic GVHD (Graph Versus Host Disease) doesn't show up.

I really can't wait for November when I can be completely back to normal. Hopefully, it will come as fast as the 100 days did.

Love,
Karina

GVHD often occurs after transplants and can cause a variety of problems ranging from bothersome to life-threatening. We were blessed in that Karina never suffered from GVHD. Her sister's stem cells were actually a perfect match. Her body accepted them as her own.

3/3/0?

I can't believe we go home tomorrow!!! I've been packing, geez, I've accumulated a ton of crap. It's taking me forever to figure out where to put things. I'm taking a break right now, I just filled up my whole bag, its gonna be really heavey. The last 3monthes have flown by, I feel like I blinked and it was over, which I'm glad of. It will really nice to be back at home in Gig Harbor and start to get back in the swing of things. I'm so thankful everything is going well, I really hope the chronic GVHD doesnt show up.

I really can't wait for November when I can be completely back to normal, hopefully it will come as fast as the 100 days did.

Love,
Karine

131

Chapter 12: Three Perfect Years

In April, shortly after we returned to Gig Harbor, Karina and Karl Nielsen, a boy she had liked since fifth grade, began dating. They had been friends since 8th grade, but now he actually *liked* her in return. She was thrilled. Karl had some of Karina's girlfriends over to help him make a big poster inviting her to be his girlfriend. Later in the week, the girls hung the poster in the window of Karina's bedroom, which faced our driveway. The goal was for Karina to see this invite when she walked out to his car that evening. However, it was dark by then, and we thought the plan had failed. Just then one of the girl's dads drove down the driveway with his lights shining. It illuminated the poster, and Karina was able to read his request. After wondering in the hospital if anyone would ever like her, here he was - the boy of her dreams. They dated and had fun hanging out together throughout the rest of their high school years. Her fears of not going to dances with someone special were put to rest as she went to many dances with Karl throughout this time. To see him return the feelings and show care toward our girl seemed like another little touch of God's love toward her.

Karina writes in her prayer journal:

Thanks for what's going on in my life. It really is awesomely amazing. I mean he is wonderful. Is anyone else in this world like him? I don't think so! He's so on fire for YOU and so sweet...

Although there continued to be needed check-ups with the doctor, overall her blood work remained very good. She could not go back to school, however, as her immune system was pretty well depleted, and she was too vulnerable. As a mom this always worried me of course, but seeing her enjoying life and friends put me at ease.

During that time Karina and I did everything together. Determined to stay on top of school work, she took online courses and worked very hard on her academics. She went on errands with me and to the Bellevue club every week and joined in on lunches with my lady friends. We had such a great time together. They were precious shared hours that remain a treasured memory for me.

By November 2007, it was her junior year, and she was finally able to go back to school. It was wonderful to see her enjoying life as a normal teenager.

Summer came and she got to attend Malibu as a camper for the first time, which was a real highlight. Our family enjoyed our annual vacations to Roche Harbor and Malibu, and we felt great joy watching Karina spend hours wake boarding and water skiing in the serene Princess Louisa Inlet. We thoroughly enjoyed these days. The worst seemed behind us, and I dared to believe our family and life would be normal from here on out.

She was beyond happy to enter school for her senior year and joined the swim team where she earned a varsity letter. For her senior project she walked a half marathon with five friends and raised $5,000 for the Fred Hutch. She also made welcome bags for kids who, like her, are diagnosed with cancer for the first time. These were then delivered to the pediatric cancer clinic to be distributed to children on their first scary night in the hospital. Since she loved kids, she also spent many hours volunteering with the children's ministry at Chapel Hill Church where her former kindergarten teacher, Deb Robertson, was now the Children's Director. In addition, she was the high school Young Life leader for middle school kids and they loved her.

To the amazement of many around her, Karina graduated high school with her class in June of 2009. Despite missing many days throughout her high school experience, she was still able to graduate with honors and earned more than one scholarship. In fact one of her counselors gave a glowing letter of recommendation that summarizes Karina's resolve and the inspiration she was to the educators around her.

"...there are times in an educator's life when you pause to wonder who taught whom and who taught the most valuable lessons. Such is the case with Karina Robertson. Gig Harbor High School taught her academics which hopefully will broaden her understanding of the world and open doors for the future. Karina taught us that courage can come in a 95 lb girl, losing hair, pale as pale can be and so tired even thinking was at times too much. Karina taught us that to succeed one can overcome unbelievable obstacles such as pain, nausea, frightening medical procedures and isolation. Karina demonstrated strength in surmounting these obstacles not just once but twice. I hope we taught Karina half as much as she taught us. I hope I will be

able to use the lessons she has taught me about courage, determination and grace. I certainly had an excellent teacher."

Kyle Lytle

Karl had been accepted at Northwest University in Kirkland, and he really wanted Karina to attend there as well. Although she was more interested in Seattle Pacific University, she was swayed to follow him at first. But in April of 2009, they broke up and those plans changed. With a two week application deadline looming, she hurriedly applied to Seattle Pacific University and was accepted. Although they got back together over the summer, she went ahead with her decision to attend SPU. We were really happy as we had always wanted her to go where she really wanted.

I remember her last summer, 2009, very fondly. Karina was feeling great, and we lived life to the fullest. For her senior trip we hosted her special circle of friends on board *Epiphany* for an excursion to Victoria. It was such fun to see her celebrating with the girls who had meant so much to her over the past years.

She also thoroughly enjoyed our usual family activities. We had invited both sets of our families to join us at Roche Harbor for the Fourth of July that year. Our time together was filled with love, laughter and great memories. There is always a run in the harbor on the Fourth of July in which our family participates. In fact, the next year when we were back at Roche Harbor for the first time without her, I was so pleased to discover a photograph in town of Karina between Ron and me at the finish line with all of our families behind us. It seemed providential that we had gathered the extended family together for one last time.

After Roche Harbor, we of course traveled up to Malibu and enjoyed one of the best times ever. The weather, which can often be gray and rainy in early July, was picture perfect: warm and sunny with blue skies overhead. Karina wake boarded every day in the inlet and just loved it. We also got to meet and listen to a family favorite, singer Brandon Heath, when he performed for us and two other boating families. It was a real treat to be given an intimate concert out at the Beyond Malibu base camp. Karina loved meeting him and listening to his music in the context of one of her most cherished places. It seemed the world was smiling upon Karina and blessing her with joy during what would be her last summer season on this earth. It was also a rich family time and will remain in my memory forever as the best summer of my entire life.

Those three years following the transplant were a priceless gift, and we were filled with gratitude to God for the medical advances that extended her life.

FROM KARINA'S PRAYER JOURNAL
about her first boyfriend
at age 16

Karina prays to the Lord:

Thanks for what's going on in my life, it really is awesomely amazing. I mean he is wonderful, is anyone else in the world like him? I don't think so! He's so on fire for You, and so sweet...

Top photo, opposite page: The day Karl Nielsen asked Karina to be his girlfriend (with the help of Karina's friends and sister), when he gave her a rose the color of the sunset.

Lower photo, opposite page: Sunset at Roche Harbor, the weekend she received her first kiss.

Sketch by Katie.

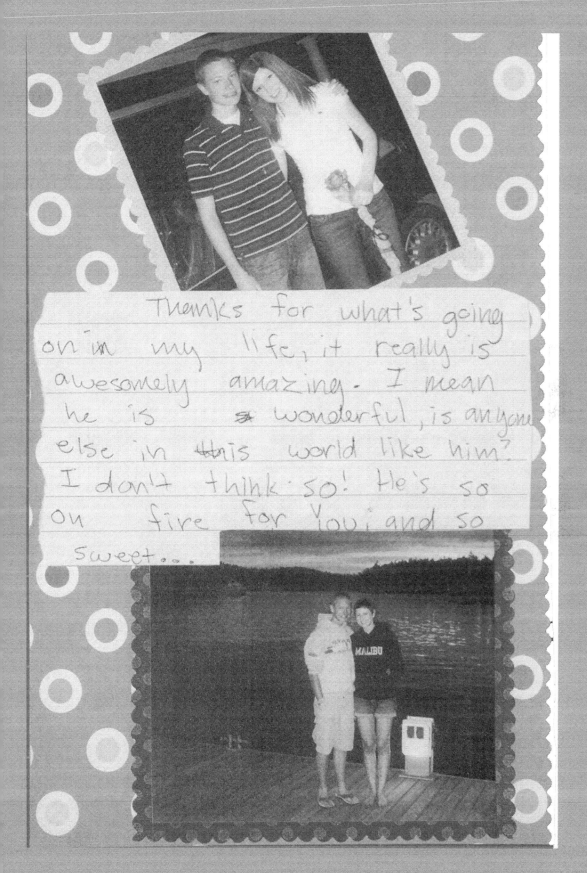

Thanks for what's going on in my life, it really is awesomely amazing. I mean he is so wonderful, is anyone else in this world like him? I don't think so! He's so on fire for you; and so sweet...

Dance

Annika Robertson

Gilbert

AP English per. 6

June 14, 2010

Seeing Sapphire

One-quarter carat sapphire sat simply on my sister's left middle finger. It was too big; the brilliant blue stone wavered right and left day in and day out, sometimes hiding under her perfect piano hands. It saw everything she saw, and now it sees everything I see. She carried it as a part of her, and now so must I.

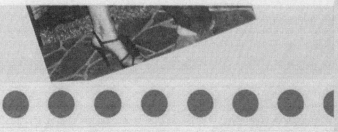

MALIBU RAPIDS

Scale 1:12 000 (49°59'N) Échelle

On your mark... get set... go!

Senior recognition

Gig Harbor High School
Varsity Athletic Award
GH

swimmer

GH

practice

Gig Harbor High School
Varsity Athletic Award
GH

SCRAPBOOK PAGE MADE BY KARINA ABOUT
HER COMMUNITY SERVICE DURING HIGH SCHOOL
FOR HER SENIOR NOTEBOOK, 2009

Because of my illness I have not been able to participate in as many activities as I would have liked to. However, I try to get involved as much as I can. I participate in a variety of ministry activities. I volunteer in the Children's Ministries Office at Chapel Hill Presbyterian Church every week. I've been volunteering there since my junior year. There I help organize Sunday school activities and do whatever the Children's Ministries Director wants me to do. I have also been a Vacation Bible School leader at Chapel Hill during the summers of 2006 and 2008; I plan to do so again this summer. At Vacation Bible School, I lead a group of about five elementary age children in discussion and various activities.

I also organized my own day camp at my home with some friends in 2006. We have been doing this project together since we were in sixth grade. For a week in the summer we lead about fifty girls in fun activities and games. We gave them a message about Jesus at the end of each day. Each day we had a creative theme, like princess day and carnival day. I had a blast with those little girls! One of them even commented, "It was the best week of my life!" In February 2008, I went on a mission trip to Mexico with my youth group at Chapel Hill. We went down to Tijuana for a week and built houses for the less fortunate. I am also a Young Life leader for the sixth grade girls at Kopachuck Middle School. I began that endeavor this fall, and have enjoyed every minute of it! I teach the girls about God, and encourage them in their faith.

Lower sketch: drawing from Katie's book about Karina as a little girl, Our Special Treasure, available on amazon.com/books.

COMMUNITY ACTIVITIES, COMMUNITY SERVICE, OR SPORTS

Because of my illness I have not been able to participate in as many activities as I would have liked to, however, I try to get involved as much as I can. I participate in a variety of ministry activities. I volunteer in the Children's Ministries Office at Chapel Hill Presbyterian Church every week. I've been volunteering there since my junior year. There I help organize Sunday school activities and do whatever the Children's Ministries Director wants me to do. I have also been a Vacation Bible School leader at Chapel Hill during the summer of 2006 and 2008; I plan to do so again this summer. At Vacation Bible School, I lead a group of about five elementary age children in discussion and various activities. I also organized my own day camp at my home with some friends in 2006. We had been doing this project together since we were in sixth grade. For a week in the summer we lead about fifty girls in fun activities and games. We gave them a message about Jesus at the end of each day. Each day we had a creative theme, like princess day and carnival day. I had a blast with those little girls! One of them even commented, "it was the best week of my life!" In February 2008 I went on a mission trip to Mexico with my youth group at Chapel Hill. We went down to Tijuana for a week and built houses for the less fortunate. I am also a Young Life leader for the sixth grade girls at Kopachuck Middle School. I began that endeavor this fall, and have enjoyed every minute of it! I teach the girls about God and encourage them in their faith.

Directing a craft at Summer Splash 2006

Summer Splash 2006

My group at VBS 2009

Building houses in Mexico 200

SI SE PUEDE
MEXICO
YES WE CAN

8

KARINA'S HALF-MARATHON SENIOR PROJECT

For Karina's senior project, she and her sister, Annika, and five of her best friends walked the Seattle half-marathon. Madeline Monson, Aundi Ragan, Chelsea Demoss, Kalei Church, and Maddie Larson walked together and had a great time. Karina raised $5,000 for the Fred Hutchinson Cancer Research Center. The best part was seeing Karina complete the thirteen miles and finish strong.

shows families make best support systems

Family helps high school senior overcome leukemia

Illustration from Annika's book, *My Sister and Me*.

Top photo: Young Life's Malibu Camp, Princess Louisa Inlet, British Columbia. Pictured are Nootka dorm and the dining hall.

Lower photo: Annika, Erik, Karina on our boat heading through the Malibu rapids.

KARINA'S PRAYER JOURNAL
AN ENTRY FROM DURING HIGH SCHOOL

Karina prays to the Lord:

Thanks again for the fabulous swim meet --- I am so glad!!!!!!!! And for the drive postponement!!!! I love you so much! And thanks for my life back (after last year). I forgot!!!!!!! Please help me finish my online stuff on time!!!

I am so worried about all that stuff. Please give me peace.

I love you and thank you for everything!!!!!!!!!!!
Love,
Karina

Karina was so thankful to the Lord for everything, especially for life after the transplant.

Karina was on the Gig Harbor High School swim team and loved it. She earned a varsity letter not through her competitive times, but because of her determination to participate which was recognized and respected by her teammates and coach. She was able to complete part of sophomore year and all of her senior year.

Karina brought all her worries to the Lord. Driving was a challenge, and she was so happy when she finally got her license.   The pressure of getting her schoolwork done on time so she could graduate with her classmates was also stressful. Because of her illness she had to take many of her courses independently online. No matter how she was feeling, she always tackled her coursework.

Photo: on the bow of our boat Epiphany, with Malibu in the background. Karina, Erik, Annika. Summer 2008.

Thanks again for the fabulous swim meet - I'm so glad!!!!!/!!!
And for the drive. postponement!!!!
I love so much! And thanks for my life back (after last year). I forgot!!!!!!! Please help me finish my online stuff on time!!!
I'm so worried about all that stuff, please give me peace.
I love you & thank you for evrrything!!!!!!!!!
Love,
Karina

Photo: Annika and Karina, summer 2009.
On the top of our anchored boat, where the kids love to
jump off into Princess Louisa Inlet.

Karina's Prayer Journal
March 2, 2004
Seventh grade, the year before diagnosis.

John Chapter 6

First, Jesus feeds the five thousand. Then He walks
on water. Then he talked about being the bread of life
and some people didn't understand.

I think what Jesus meant by the bread of life, is we
can't live without Him like we can't live without food,
(bread). Bread/food gives us life. Jesus also gives us
life-everlasting.

John Chapt. 6   10:18 pm   3/2/04
                                 Tues.

      First Jesus feeds the 5,000. Then He walks on water. Then He talked about being the bread of life and some people didn't understand.

      I think what Jesus meant by the bread of life is we can't live without Him, like we can't live without without food (bread). Bread/food gives us life. Jesus also gives us life — everlasting.

TIDES

Gig Harbor
High School
Graduation, Class of 2009.

Karina loved wakeboarding at Malibu. Summer 2009.

MEMORIES OF PRINCESS LOUISA INLET

Princess Louisa Inlet was a granite-walled gorge where seven thousand foot tall mountains rose from water to sky. Beyond the Malibu Rapids, the deep, clear water was as calm as a mountain lake. Snowmelt waterfalls poured and trickled down the cliffs. In the peaceful quiet, the only sounds were of falling water and my children's voices.

One of our favorite places was Chatterbox Falls, where mist hung at the base like a cloud. Once, Karina and Annika found a rock surrounded by water. They took turns sitting on it, posing as Disney's Little Mermaid.

As we took the dinghy around, we were never in a hurry. My kids dragged their toes in blue water too deep to fathom, and talked happily. Sometimes we stopped to hike, or swim. On remote beaches the kids searched for bits of sparkly granite. At night, they threw rocks into the dark water to make sparks of glowing phosphorescence.

At sunset, we would drive the dingy back to our boat on the outside of MacDonald Island, feeling satisfied with the perfect fullness of the day. In the distance, where two mountains converged, we could see Camp Malibu, the place that had brought Ron and me together when we were young.

Anchored in the inlet, most days we kayaked in inflatable kayaks. Karina and Annika especially liked to kayak around a tiny islet near where we anchored. Annika would cruise ahead, and Karina would secretly paddle up behind her and grab onto the back of her kayak. Annika would wonder why paddling was suddenly so difficult. Then Karina's laughter would carry across the inlet.

To our family, the scenery was more than just beautiful. It was sacred. Princess Louisa Inlet contained the infinite. It was our own special playground, a place to which we always returned. In its safe waters, we could relax and explore as a family, floating together in a setting so peaceful it was as if we were resting, protected, in the Lord's hand.

Karina jumping.

Malibu in the distance, where we anchor.

Tubing wars with cousins.

Karina at Chatterbox.

Annika as the Little Mermaid.

Karina, Annika, Madeline, Chelsea, and Maddie completing the Seattle half-marathon 2008.

Best friends: Karina, Aundi, Madeline, Kalei, and Chelsea.

Photo: Roche Harbor, summer 2009, with cousins from Montana. Pictured left to right: Grace, Erik, Isaac, Annika, Hannah, and Karina. Not pictured: Caleb. We were so thankful to have everyone together Karina's final summer.

Photo: Christmas 2009 with cousins. Back row left to right: Sam, Jonathan, Annika, Maddie, Karina, Makayla. Front row: David, Erik, Bo, Ben, and Matthew. Not pictured: Becky.

**Fourth of July at Roche Harbor, Summer 2009.
Running the annual race as a family.**

We found this photo the summer after we lost Karina
on the Roche Harbor website. Finding it was a special gift.
Karina is in the middle of Ron and Katie. Also pictured are
cousins (bottom row left to right) Maddie, Annika, Ben,
David, Sam, (back row) Jonathan, Katie's sister and
brother-in-law Rob and Laurie Duyker, and Erik.
Everyone participated.

Chapter 13: Final Diagnosis

Summer came to an end, and we looked forward with excitement to taking Karina to Seattle Pacific University for the beginning of her college experience. Although she was somewhat apprehensive about being in the big city, her best friend was going there as well, and she felt confident and excited about her choice. Orientation day was a great day for all of us. I bumped into my best friend from college who was there delivering her son, and one of Ron's best friend's had a daughter, Honnah Weber, who was starting there as well. It felt like a mini-reunion. Although Karina and Honnah had only met as little girls, they immediately connected as young women and became good friends. Karina came to love the college, the surrounding city of Seattle, and the new friends she was making: however, at the same time, she was often homesick. Many weekends found her back home in Gig Harbor. The trial of cancer had truly bonded us as a family, and she missed that closeness.

In October that year, while at school, Karina contracted the dreaded swine flu. Of course my fears were aroused whenever she was sick, but this time, due to the media attention, it seemed especially serious. Again, my worries were put to rest as she recovered with no problem.

At Thanksgiving she was still very healthy and having a great time at college. She was making new friends and enjoying her classes. Things with Karl continued on and off, and during one of the off times she met a wonderful young man, Mark. Although they never developed a deep relationship, his friendship and encouragement was still special to her.

On December 22, 2009, while Karina was home for Christmas break, we went to the doctor's for her six month check up. This was the longest period of time we had gone without an appointment. Although she seemed fine, I still got nervous every time as we sat awaiting the lab results. There was no cause for alarm, however, as her blood work was picture perfect. I was not only relieved, I was ecstatic. It was Christmas, and our family was together to enjoy the holiday weeks ahead with our healthy girl. As a mom, it just doesn't get much better than that. We had no idea this would be our last Christmas together. For now, we enjoyed every minute and had no reason to believe the future would be anything but bright.

When Karina returned to college after the break, she discovered Karl had transferred to SPU and had chosen to be in her dorm. In the past, she might have found this arrangement a welcome surprise, but given where she was currently in her life, she instead found it to be an added stress. He was persistent and wanted to get back together but she was not ready. She was trying to make new friends and experience all there was to take in of college living. While all was well with her physical health, emotionally she was in anguish. Like many young women her age she thought a lot about the kind of man she wanted to be with. She had experienced some new people since Karl, yet her heart kept being pulled toward him and she could not let him go. She was not at peace but remained determined to wait on the Lord continually as reflected in her journals. She knew God's plan is best and sought his wisdom in every aspect of her life, especially in regards to her romance.

At the beginning of January, right after Karina returned to college, she developed a rash and came home to see her doctor. It turned out to be minor, but the week after that she began complaining of chest pain. I picked her up on campus, and once again we trekked down to her doctor in Gig Harbor. She was convinced she had walking pneumonia. He shared her suspicions and sent her for a chest x-ray. Upon seeing a shadow on the films, he sent us immediately to Tacoma General Hospital for a cat-scan. Since it was a Friday afternoon and the emergency room was our only option, we sat waiting until nearly midnight to receive the results. Although we still took every ailment seriously, I was not expecting there to be anything gravely wrong; therefore the results were shocking. To our horror, the scan revealed a tumor on her lung. It was Friday, January 22, 2010, when she was diagnosed with cancer for the third time. Just one month after her labs had reflected perfect health, the leukemia had returned in the form of a rare chest tumor.

After we received the stark diagnosis, Ron left the hospital to go home to be with the other kids. The doctors insisted on keeping Karina overnight but could not secure a room until approximately 3 a.m., so we waited. This was our first experience in an adult hospital since she was now over age 18. Previously we had always been in the Children's hospital and been given different treatment. The first question she was asked upon admission was if she had a living will, and I could sense her defiance when she answered sharply, "I don't need one!"

Finally we were checked in and given both a room and hospital issued pajamas to get comfortable. But comfort was the last thing we felt. Given our history, one would think we would be used to dreadful news from doctors, but this time we were especially unprepared. She had enjoyed three years of good health since the transplant and just one month earlier, her blood work had been perfect. This news was completely unexpected and really caught us off guard.

The darkness of the night seemed to match the state of my heart and soul. I could sense Karina, too, felt overwhelmed and scared. I crawled up into the single bed, cupped myself around her, and whispered, "There is nothing we can do now…we are in God's hands. He will take us where He wants us to go." The words were barely off my lips when an undeniable presence descended upon us. It was like a heavy wool blanket of peace and love had been laid over us. I knew it was God. I was cupped around Karina as we were both covered by His awesome, loving hand. Amid the thick darkness, His goodness prevailed. The spirit of the living God was hovering over the void of our fear and I knew we would be safe no matter what. Trusting God is like that: being cupped in His hand. He carries us wherever He wants to go and He loves us so much we do not have to fear, only nestle in for the ride. That feeling, of being held by our heavenly Father, who cared immensely about every detail of our lives, gave us hope to face the future. I do not know how I would have navigated the next dark chapter had it not been for that gift of feeling His very real presence in that mid-night moment.

Photo: Katie, Karina, and Ron at Seattle Pacific University's parent orientation.

A NOTE TO KARINA FROM KATIE ON HER FIRST NIGHT IN THE DORM
September 23, 2009

Hi Karina!

Happy 1st night in the dorm! I am <u>so</u> excited for you, and so very proud of you! You are one <u>very</u> special girl with a <u>very</u> special purpose! The Lord has AMAZING plans for you. Always keep your eyes on Him and BELIEVE he has you in His hands! I love you <u>so</u> much Karina. I miss you already --- there is a presence about you that is <u>so</u> unique and special --- truly the Lord shining thru you! Be confident... Joshua 1:8-9. Be <u>BOLD</u> and be <u>STRONG</u> for the Lord thy God is with you...Do <u>NOT</u> be Afraid, Do NOT be dismayed...walk in faith and victory! You will always be my special treasure --- I treasure every memory with you! I look forward to so many MORE!

9/23/09

Hi Karina!
happy 1st night in the dorm ☺ I am so excited for you and so very proud of you! You are one very special girl w/ a very special purpose! The Lord has AMAZING plans for you! Always keep your eyes on Him and BELIEVE he has you in His hands! I love you so much Karii

I miss you already ~ there is a presence about you that is so unique + special - truly the Lord shining thru you! Be confident... Joshua 1:8-9
☆ Be BOLD + Be STRONG for the Lord thy God is w/ you... DO NOT be Afraid, DO NOT be dismayed... walk in faith + victory! You will always be my special treasure - I treasure every memory w/ you! I look forward to so many MORE! Can't wait (back)

KARINA'S PRAYER JOURNAL
FALL, 2009

FRESHMAN YEAR AT
SEATTLE PACIFIC UNIVERSITY

Thank you that I ended up here Lord. It feels so right, so meant to be. Thank you for getting me here. I love you.

Photo: Karina, her friend Honnah Weber, and Madeline Monson. This photo was at SPU's college-wide crazy Christmas sweater event. Karina was blessed with great friends at SPU. Karina and Madeline were best friends since before they started kindergarten. They did everything together, including spending all of their childhood birthdays together. Honnah was a special friend whose family were missionaries in the Ukraine who reconnected with Karina at SPU.

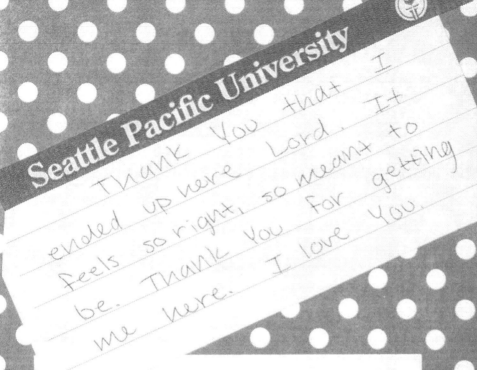

Seattle Pacific University

Thank You that I ended up here Lord. It feels so right, so meant to be. Thank You for getting me here. I love you.

THE FALCON

'She hung onto Phil. 4:13'

Floor inspired by Robertson

by Melissa Steffan
assistant news editor

On Monday morning, former SPU freshman Karina Robertson, 19, died at Tacoma General Hospital as the result of pneumonia after complications due to treatment for leukemia.

Robertson withdrew from Seattle Pacific at the beginning of Winter Quarter after she was diagnosed with leukemia, but remained an integral part of her floor in Emerson Hall.

"She was beautiful and funny and she loved God," said sophomore Katie Rose, Second East Emerson student ministry coordinator. "She was just trying to figure out her life and where she belonged at SPU."

This was the third time Robertson had been diagnosed

KARINA'S PRAYER JOURNAL
SEATTLE PACIFIC UNIVERSITY 2009

God, please help me...I love You and You've brought me so far. I know you won't let go. I <u>need</u> and <u>want</u> to focus on YOU. I keep losing it. I hate all this anxiety and worry. It doesn't constantly need to be there. I need some peace somehow.

Karina had alot on her mind, as most college students do, but told me that she was going to rest in the Lord and that she trusted Him with everything.

Photo: Karina enjoying college life, making cupcakes with friends. The decorations on the cupcakes are ballerinas, which is why Karina is posing.

This was Karina's last journal entry.

God please help me... I love you and You've brought me so far I know YOU won't let go.

I need & want to focus on YOU. I keep losing it. I hate all this anxiety and worry, it doesn't constantly need to be there. I need some peace somehow

Chapter 14: Facing the Enemy

We went home the next day to get ready for her treatment. We knew this was serious and that we were headed back into a fight, but the doctors gave us three days at home to make preparations. The next day, Saturday, was a big dance for Annika, and we had to switch gears and focus on her. Of course it felt strange to be preparing simultaneously for a battle and a dance, but this is how life is sometimes. Even in the midst of the serious, there are moments of joy that cannot be ignored. We had learned the importance of balancing not only the needs of all of our children, but also the many other facets of our life. We tried not to let the illness take over.

Amid the flurry of polished nails, fancy hair styles, and beautiful dresses, other parents arrived to take photos of our glamorous girls and their dates. These were new friends and most had no idea what Karina had been through in her life or what had transpired in the last 24 hours. It was surreal: one of our girls was shining that night while the other, was dying. Over the next few days we attempted normalcy while facing the looming prospect of another stay at Fred Hutch. I had been dealing with vertigo, and it got worse that week. I felt dizzy whenever I stood up. I found myself humming the tune to the old hymn "On Christ the solid rock I stand" as a way of reminding myself of the sure foundation on which I was standing despite the fuzzy feeling in my head. Karina must have heard me for she exclaimed, "Oh mom, I love that song. We have been singing it at college during chapel, and I just love knowing that Jesus is the rock on which we stand!"

We stood together on that rock as we faced the trials ahead.

Karina would need a lymphocyte infusion to fight the tumor since her own white cells were not doing the job. Karina's body had not developed the ability to fight back against the cancer, and a relapse had occurred. We would need to take her back to the Fred Hutch, but first she needed to undergo two rounds of chemotherapy to attempt remission. After consults with the Fred Hutch it was decided we would complete these at Tacoma General near our Gig Harbor home, rather than relocate the family again.

Right before we went back to the hospital to begin the treatments, Bill Duppenthaler, the Young Life area director from Gig Harbor, coordinated a prayer meeting on our behalf. Close to 300 people joined in to pray for Karina and our family. It felt as if we were the warriors going into battle surrounded by a rally of support. This prayer meeting really strengthened us and left us feeling full of peace as we forged ahead. I still felt confident in the promise the Lord had given me: "This sickness would not end in death."

Karina and I went together to Tacoma General for five days of chemotherapy. Like before, either Ron or I stayed with her continuously so that she was never alone. While one of us stayed the night, the other went home for precious sleep and connection with the other kids. The treatments went very smoothly with no infections. We felt the power of those many prayers and praised God for giving all of us strength: physically, spiritually, and emotionally.

We knew her hair, which had just reached the length it had been in 8th grade prior to her first diagnosis, would be falling out by about week two. I did some quick research and found a man who came to our home, shaved her head, and then fashioned a wig out of her own hair. It was perfect and she was so happy to "keep" her own hair.

It was now February and with the first treatment over, she came home to Gig Harbor to recover. Although she missed her college friends, she was relieved not to have homework. We had withdrawn her from winter quarter classes and had made the trek up to campus to empty her dorm room. The girls on her floor there were so sad it confused me. They seemed to think Karina would never return, while I was full of hope she would be back by spring. It was heartbreaking to see their sorrow. In a short time they had all become so bonded. Even Karina and her roommate, who had at first seemed like a polar opposites, had grown to be good friends. We were so blessed to feel the support of these wonderful young women.

During her recovery at home, Karina mostly slept or worked on a collage she was making of things she liked and dreams for the future. Friends would come to visit, or we would watch movies together as a family. She and Annika would sit on Karina's bed coloring like little girls and watching sappy made-for-television movies. They just loved being together and enjoyed their precious time. As a family, we tried to keep things as normal as possible. We had been through this routine and knew what to do. Every week she was checked to see how her blood counts were progressing. When the bone marrow production reached a certain level, she was ready for round two.

When March arrived, Karina and I again went to Tacoma General for her second treatment. This time I could not help feeling things were different. As the nurse hooked her up to various medications and the chemotherapy, she shook her head and commented she had never seen this combination used before. I had a sick feeling in my stomach. Knowing the cancer to be an evil enemy, I wanted to face it down and kill it and thus consented to whatever weapons the professionals advised. Yet, at the same time, I knew full well the damage it would do to the good cells in her body. Essentially, we were consenting to "friendly fire" in an effort to kill the intruder.

KARINA'S COLLAGE OF HER FAVORITE THINGS

Karina made this collage right before we went to the hospital for the last time. She loved scrapbooking, and found it relaxing to create this colorful collage about things she loved.

KATIE'S PRAYER JOURNAL
APRIL 2010
IN THE HOSPITAL WITH KARINA

Encouraging verses that I wrote in my journal.

Psalm 41

Blessed is he who has regard for the weak;
The Lord delivers him in times of trouble;
The Lord will protect him and preserve his life;
He will bless him in the land and not surrender him
to the desire of his foes.

The Lord will sustain him on his sickbed
and restore him from his bed of illness.

Have mercy on me --- heal me!

But you Oh Lord, have mercy on me, for my enemy
doesn't triumph over me.
In my integrity, you uphold me and set me in your
presence forever.
Praise be to you, Oh Lord!

Psalm 28

The Lord is my strength and shield. Our hearts trust in
Him and will be helped! My heart leaps for joy. I give
thanks to Him --- the Lord is the strength of his people
a fortress of salvation for his annointed one. Save us ---
bless your inheritance.
Be our shepherd and carry us forever!

Blessed is he who has
regard for the weak; the
Lord delivers him in
times of trouble;
the Lord will protect him
and preserve his life;
he will bless him in
the land and not surrender
him to the desire of his
foes.
The Lord will sustain him
on his sickbed and
restore him from his
bed of illness.

have mercy on me ~ heal
me!

but you oh Lord, have
mercy on me, for my
enemy doesn't triumph
over me. In my integrity
you uphold me + set me
in your presence forever.
Praise be to you O Lord!

Psalm 41

Psalm 28

the Lord is my strength
and shield!
our ♡ trust in Him and
will be helped!
My ♡ leaps for JOY I
will give thanks to Him –
the Lord is the strength
of His people a fortress
of salvation for His
anointed one
save us – bless your
inheritance
be our shepherd +
carry us forever!

April 6, 2010

O Lord,

Please heal us...We will wait on You. Deliver us from
this ordeal --- bring us home to our house soon --- we will
wait on You, Lord. We love you, and always will --- we
want to tell of your loving-kindness and your wonders
that we will bring glory to You. Continue to hear our
prayer --- we do cry out to you and love you with all our
hearts! Rescue us --- that we may live long lives to
declare your mighty power and unfailing love!

                                        Amen

The Lord is with us --- I will <u>NOT</u> be afraid! The Lord
is with us. He is our HELPER! I will look in triumph on
my enemies!

We will trust in the Lord.

Name of the Lord --- cut them (cancer) off!
The Lord is my strength and song.

4/6/10

O Lord,
please heal us...
we will wait on you
deliver us from this
ordeal & bring us home
to our house soon—
we will wait on you Lord.
we love you and
always will— we want
to tell of your loving-
kindness and your
wonders that we will
bring glory to you!
continue to hear
our prayer— we do
cry out to you and
love you w/ all our
♡, Rescue us— that
we may live long
lives to declare your
mighty power +
unfailing love!
Amen.

the Lord is with us—
I will NOT be afraid!
the Lord is w/ us He
is our HELPER!
i will look in triumph
on my enemies!
We will trust in the Lord

Name of the Lord— cut
them off!
the Lord is my strength +
song!

175

Chapter 15: Anchored Until the End

We had been home after the second treatment for about a week when Karina came down with a fever, and we knew we had to take her in to get checked out. As a family we had been watching the "Lost" series and when it was over that evening we packed up and prepared to return to the hospital. She knew the routine and gathered up her favorite security blanket, some movies, and a few books into her backpack for what she knew could be another hospital stay. I was so weary of the hospital and really did not want to return. I had come to simply hate it there. Despite the kindness of the staff, I did not want what it represented. I wanted to be home in our peaceful house by the sea with my healthy family by my side. I wanted to throw a temper tantrum, but Karina just took it in stride. Back to the ER we went to await a room and more medical intervention.

It was quickly determined she had developed pneumonia. Over the next few days she lost her appetite and began getting weaker. We would leave the kids with her while Ron and I went to dinner bringing her back some food in hopes that if we brought her something from a favorite restaurant, she would eat. But little by little she grew weaker and worse. Dr. Thomas remained optimistic that her bone marrow would soon start coming back up, and with it, her immune system. This had happened before. She would get a little sick, but then the marrow, which is the factory in the body that produces white blood cells, would kick into gear igniting the immune system to fight the infection. Every day we waited for the labs to reflect an improvement in her system, and every day I would be frustrated at the lack of improvement. Her marrow was not recovering. One day while driving to the hospital, I heard a song on the radio about waiting on the Lord. I realized I had placed my hope on the lab results rather than on the Lord and needed to shift my focus. It was difficult this time, as the prayers I was praying were not being answered like they had before. It was also around this time that I heard His voice alerting me to the possibility this was not going to end the way I wanted. He was asking if I would still trust in Him. This is the moment where faith is truly tested. When we do not get our own way in the world and things do not make sense the question always comes down to this: will we walk by faith and not by sight? We can make a plan for our whole life, but things outside the realm of our control will inevitably occur. It is how we handle those times that determine our character.

"Many are the plans in a man's heart but it is the Lord's purpose that prevails." Proverbs 19:21

We reached the day when Karina needed to have an oxygen mask. This had also happened the first time she had pneumonia, so we were not entirely hopeless. We still thought it would all change soon and we would get to go home. But she only got worse. When she started to vomit blood, they moved her to the critical care floor. I huddled in the corner, fearful and in great dismay, but she remained strong and even said to me, "Mom, if Jesus can sweat blood, then I can barf it." Her grace and fortitude in the midst of all she had to endure was truly inspiring. A scripture she held to and followed was Philippians 4:13:

"I can do all things through Christ who strengthens me"

We celebrated Easter in the hospital with her and watched the *Sound of Music,* which was her favorite movie. This time was not the same though. She was more tired and less conversational. She did not seem herself. Her health and her strength were failing and I was ever fearful they would say she needed to be moved to the ICU.

That night came in a most confusing way. The nurses had come into the room at around 2 a.m. and told me things were stable, but then at 4 a.m. they returned to say a move to the ICU was needed immediately. We had to awaken and pack everything up right away. We were both perturbed to say the least. I was annoyed, not only that we were being forced to move in the middle of the night but that we were being told once again she needed the ICU. First off, we had been in there before when she had pneumonia the first time and almost lost her, and I dreaded having to face that possibility again. And secondly, I did not want to believe she had deteriorated to that point and thus was fighting the move. As they rolled her bed down the dim hallway the IV pole loomed like a cross above her. I dragged along side with our bags of belongings in hand, overcome with a sense of doom. The hallway closed in around us like a long suffocating tunnel, steadily stealing our life with every step. I clutched at the hope of recovery but feared death could be awaiting us beyond the doors.

When a doctor came in the next day saying the marrow had actually come up my first thought was, *I told you so.* I so wanted to believe all the hassle of the midnight move had been for naught and she was really fine. Ron and I went out and celebrated with friends at a restaurant however, before long, she worsened. Over the next few days we rode a roller coaster of emotions - one minute celebrating what seemed like a victory only to have it dashed the next minute with more bad news.

On her second night in the ICU, Ron was staying with her while I went home to sleep. At about one in the morning he called and said with urgency, "Katie get here quick!" I sped to the hospital where Ron told me things had taken a turn for the worst. Her breathing had become so labored she needed to be on the ventilator. He knew I would want to see and talk to her before this occurred, as he feared it could be my last chance. When I reached her bedside she lifted her slender, beautiful hands to my face and pulled it down close to hers as she whispered in a weak voice, "I love you mommy." Those were the last words I heard her speak as her questioning eyes met mine in a tender final moment of intimacy. I knew I needed to be strong amid my own fear and responded confidently, "Karina, you need this to help you get better. Everything will be alright." Then Ron and I were asked to leave the room, and I had to pry myself away from her side. I was trying to muster strength, but inside I was sick with the pain of watching her life drain away. We later saw the doctor come out of the room crying.

Once she got hooked up all we could do was wait and watch. At one point, Dr. Thomas asked to do a bone marrow test. We consented since she had been sedated for a while. We both left the hospital to do a few things and deeply regretted it after the fact. During this time she had awoken, pulled the ventilator out of her mouth and asked for us. The nurse told her we would be right back and then immediately re-inserted the ventilator. That was the last time she was conscious.

We did not leave her side after that. They gave us a whole room at the end of the hall where we set up a cot and some chairs like soldiers in the trenches. We were with her around the clock and continually poured out desperate pleas to God for the life of our girl. During the day a few friends would come and sit with us and Erin Marshall, a former Young Life kid we had mentored, would join as at night and stay for hours. Their presence was truly a blessing.

The second week in ICU her blood counts dropped drastically. The staff told us this was not good. They knew she did not have long, and this was their way of telling us. I held onto the hope her bone marrow would recover, but on Sunday, April 25th the doctor told us to gather family around as Karina was barely holding on. Our friend Rob Lane came to be with us. As a retired oncologist, he knows when the end is near and took me into one of the little alcoves for a heart to heart chat. In a very kind way he was trying to tell us that sometimes the Lord does not answer our prayers the way we want. He said Karina was in the waiting room of heaven and gently suggested we needed to let her go.

She made it through one more night. Early the next morning, April 26, Annika and Erik, who were staying next door in a place for families called the Tree House, arrived to say their final tearful good-byes to a sister they dearly loved and admired. We surrounded Karina's bed and read aloud from *God Calling*, her favorite devotional book. The entry for that day gave us great comfort as it contained one of her favorite verses.

Philippians 4:13:

> *"I can do all things through Christ who strengthens me."*

Karina had touched each of us in so many ways. She had truly been a gift from God: a blessing and joy in life and an example of courage and grace in the face of death. In a final, incredibly touching gesture, Annika bent over sister, whom she so adored, and whispered "Karina, I hope we'll get to share a room in heaven."

We continued by her side, but as the morning progressed, it became more and more evident she was slipping away. In those final moments she was just a body being kept alive by technology. Although the spirit of Karina was gone, I could not stop kissing her face. To think our sweet girl was no longer with us was heart wrenching. I could not let go. Ron and I both stood crying and crying. I could actually hardly stand, and was stooped over her unable to stop wailing. In those final moments, the grief was so deep, but at the same time, we knew she was gone and would not want us to linger. As we left for home, we cried all the way out of the building. We were confident Karina would have wanted distance put between us and the hospital as soon as possible.

I drove home, heartbroken over the loss of my treasured daughter, but as I pulled into our driveway, I also felt an inexplicable calm. Jesus had promised a peace that passes all understanding in the midst of our circumstances, and I was feeling it right at that moment. The battle was over. There was no more to be done. I knew where Karina was, and that she was finally free from this long, painful, agonizing ordeal. We knew we would now have to face the rest of our lives without her, but with our shared hope in Christ, we knew we would be together again someday.

Chapter 16: Rocks and Rainbows

We planned Karina's memorial service for May 10 in Gig Harbor and estimated 500 people would attend. Instead, to our amazement, 1,400 people came, which left standing room only in the church. I was nervous about how it would turn out. We had planned it so fast, and I didn't know what to expect. I felt I had to be the hospitality person as there were so many people we had not seen for some time.

Remembering how Karina had resonated with the song "On Christ the solid rock I stand," we added it to the program, and gave out small rocks in little bags tied with a navy blue polka dot ribbon, her favorite design, like party favors. I wanted the people who knew and loved her to have a remembrance of her. She had embodied the words of Psalms 62:5-8:

"Find rest, Oh my soul, in God alone; my hope comes from Him. He alone is my rock and my salvation, He is my fortress, I will not be shaken. My salvation and my honor depend on God. He is my mighty rock and my refuge. Trust in Him at all times, Oh people; pour out your hearts to Him for God is a refuge."

I wanted them to recall her strong faith and character but also her fun-loving spirit. When her friends shared at the memorial these were, indeed, the things of which they spoke. They described her as the instigator, always full of ideas for how to have fun. She had the ability to corral people into making her plans happen, but no one seemed to mind as she had an adventurous spirit and the ideas were always creative.

I need not have worried about how it would go. The service went perfectly with many people inspired by the life and faith of our daughter. Still today people who attended her service comment on how meaningful it was. They were either changed or at least prompted to think more deeply about faith issues. Few were left untouched.

Our family believed in a great God, and to honor that belief, during the service, we sang the song "How Great is our God." Truthfully all I could think about was, *What are people going to think?* At present, God did not seem so great. When sad things happen in life, God's character is always called into question. We wonder: is He still a loving God even when the inexplicable happens? When loved ones get hurt or sick or die? Despite my unanswered questions, I still remained convinced of His loving character.

My inspiration, Henrietta Mears had described "the veil between the present and the hereafter…as being so very, very thin." (pg. 334 of Dream Big) I knew at the moment while we were singing this song on earth, having to accept by faith what our limited sight could not see, Karina was actually witnessing, in heaven, a God greater than we could ever imagine.

In the Old Testament story of Noah, God gave a rainbow as a symbol of his presence and promise. Now, we too became the recipients of this icon of hope. At the most desperate times, when I have been at my lowest point, a rainbow has appeared to give me comfort. Again, some people may see it only as coincidence; however to me, it has happened too many times to be simply just that.

For instance, on the day Karina died Annika saw a double rainbow after we left the hospital, but this was only the beginning of the "rainbow sightings." Shortly thereafter, on the day of her memorial, many friends commented on seeing a huge rainbow while driving out of Gig Harbor after the service.

No parent ever wants to contemplate where they will lay their deceased child, but it is one of those details we had to face. I had to keep reminding myself the remains of Karina were just that, her spirit was still alive with the Lord. Despite the painfulness of the decision, we easily chose her two favorite destinations, Roche Harbor and Malibu, to be her final resting places on earth.

On Memorial Day weekend we took our pastor friend Rick Enloe and his wife Marvalee along with us on *Epiphany* to Roche Harbor. This historic seaside town held such a special place in our hearts, and we knew Karina would have been happy with our decision. We chose a special tree in the beautiful gardens where Karina had always hoped to get married and gathered around early in the morning to scatter her ashes. Later that day, as it was Memorial Day, the town hosted a parade. There were people dressed up as Civil War soldiers and mourners with bagpipes playing as well. One woman in particular was dressed all in black and went into the little chapel to kneel at the altar. It seemed oddly fitting. Townspeople who had come to know us from all the summer visits, along with a handful of good friends and family from the greater Puget Sound area, then gathered in the quaint white chapel. There, Rick led us in a small memorial service. Afterward, we hosted a reception on the grounds of the grand old 1800's estate overlooking the harbor. A beautiful venue with a huge outdoor fireplace, Karina and I had always imagined her wedding reception being held here. Now it served a very sad and different purpose as we gathered at dusk to watch the color guard from town take down the flags. Hearing of Karina, they made mention of her life and memory. No sooner had the words been spoken when a huge rainbow appeared across the harbor from one end to the other and directly over the steeple of the little church. It was the most amazing sight, especially as it had been a perfectly clear day with no rain whatsoever. We, of course, took it as another reminder of the presence of God.

We now fly into Roche Harbor every spring on the anniversary of her passing. For the past two years as we have approached the harbor, a full rainbow has appeared in the clouds. This sight always confirms that everything is alright with Karina. It gives us great comfort.

In June, right after the Memorial Day service at Roche Harbor, the four of us went to Hawaii for some much-needed rest and relaxation. We discovered it is known as the Rainbow State, and every day we saw magnificent rainbows. Then, in July, my nephew Sam came to visit us in Gig Harbor. As we sat on the deck enjoying the perfect ending to a sunny summer day, I wistfully wished aloud that we could see a rainbow. I was missing Karina so much. One minute I would be feeling alright while the next I felt I could crumble under the weight of my grief. For some reason, these rainbow sightings served as a reminder that she was not dead, only gone on ahead of us. Ron, not yet convinced of God's hand in these spontaneous displays which brought me deep comfort, thought to himself, *Yeah, right, rainbows and unicorns just appear out of the blue on sunny evenings*. But the words were barely out of my mouth when my nephew exclaimed and pointed out over the water, "Like that one?" And we all turned to see a huge rainbow rising out of our boat buoy and stretching across the horizon. The buoy appeared at the bottom like a pot of gold. Ron and Sam were both amazed and could not deny the timing while I thanked God once again for His loving-kindness to us.

Later that month we took some of Karina's ashes to Malibu. This place, so meaningful to our whole family, had greatly impacted Karina's short life, and we knew we wanted her to rest there as well. Our dear Young Life friends Pat and Laura Rhodes accompanied us. We knew if anyone understood our pain, they did. Years earlier they had experienced a double loss when their two adorable little girls, Jennifer and Jessica, had been killed in a tragic car accident. Our girls had all been friends when young and had played together at Malibu staff assignments in the past. Their daughters' ashes are also at Malibu near a kids' playground established in their honor. We chose to place Karina's ashes at Flag point near a big boulder surrounded by gorgeous hydrangea bushes. It seemed the perfect spot for our girl who trusted God as her rock and fortress. Recently, dear friends, Rob and Suzanne Lane and Chap and Dee Clark, also donated a pair of benches to Malibu as a memorial to Karina. They sit overlooking the beautiful rapids and inlet and have been host to many deeply meaningful conversations over the past few years.

The first Christmas season without Karina was especially difficult. We were all missing her dearly. On December 23rd we went to El Gaucho for dinner. As one of our favorite family restaurants, it seemed an appropriate spot to commemorate the season together as a newly formed family of four. Unwittingly we were seated at a table for five, and immediately, I felt the familiar ache of her absence. I secretly wished for a rainbow. *How silly to even ask for it,* I thought. *We are inside, and it is night time.* Even so, I said aloud, "Oh, if only we had a rainbow." As if on cue, the pianist began playing "Somewhere over the Rainbow." I was absolutely shocked to hear this song played when wintery carols were the expected music of the season. In awe, I realized that even here, inside a restaurant filled with Christmas decor, God had provided a rainbow to comfort me. Months later we had the privilege of meeting the owner of El Gaucho, since he, too, visits Roche Harbor in the summer. When I told him the story he was visibly touched. What many would attribute as mere coincidence was getting more and more difficult to ignore as evidence of the loving hand of God.

KARINA JEAN ROBERTSON
September 6, 1990 - April 26, 2010

Our sweet Karina Jean Robertson went home to be with the Lord on April 26, 2010. Born September 6, 1990, Karina lived a life of faith, love, and joy. Though only 19 years old, she accomplished much and touched many.

She battled leukemia three different times from age 14 on, with treatment including a stem cell transplant from her sister. Through her determination and hard work, Karina still graduated on time with honors from Gig Harbor High School in 2009. She was honored by the community as a Student of Distinction for overcoming adversity. While in high school, she was a member of the Varsity Swim Team and served as a middle school Young Life Leader. Karina then went on to attend Seattle Pacific University where she excelled in both academics and college life. She aspired to be an elementary school teacher.

Karina loved spending time with her family and friends. She also enjoyed reading, scrapbooking, swimming, and movie nights with her sister. Boating trips to Roche Harbor and Malibu were special memories. Karina loved children and organized camps for little girls each summer with her sister and friends. She truly put others first, and shared her love for the Lord and her kindness with all she knew.

Karina's strong faith and vibrant personality made her shine bright for all of those around her. Always thoughtful and fun, she was a treasured daughter, sister, and friend. She was preceded in death by Grammie Jean, and Karina is survived by her parents, Ron and Katie Robertson, her siblings Annika and Erik, and many adoring family members and friends.

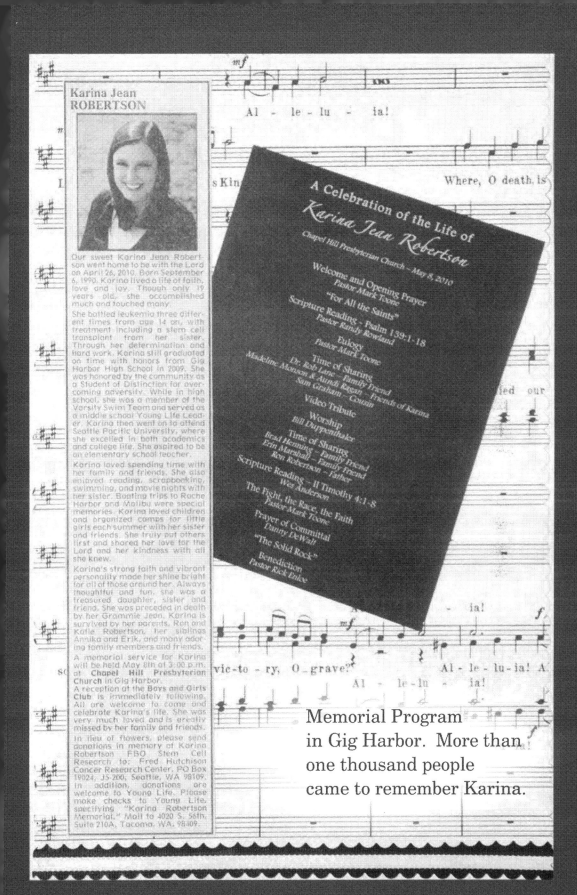

Karina Jean ROBERTSON

Our sweet Karina Jean Robertson went home to be with the Lord on April 26, 2010. Born September 6, 1990, Karina lived a life of faith, love and joy. Though only 19 years old, she accomplished much and touched many.

She battled leukemia three different times from age 14 on, with treatment including a stem cell transplant from her sister. Through her determination and hard work, Karina still graduated on time with honors from Gig Harbor High School in 2009. She was honored by the community as a Student of Distinction for overcoming adversity. While in high school, she was a member of the Varsity Swim Team and served as a middle school Young Life Leader. Karina then went on to attend Seattle Pacific University, where she excelled in both academics and college life. She aspired to be an elementary school teacher.

Karina loved spending time with her family and friends. She also enjoyed reading, scrapbooking, swimming, and movie nights with her sister. Boating trips to Roche Harbor and Malibu were special memories. Karina loved children and organized camps for little girls each summer with her sister and friends. She truly put others first and shared her love for the Lord and her kindness with all she knew.

Karina's strong faith and vibrant personality made her shine bright for all of those around her. Always thoughtful and fun, she was a treasured daughter, sister and friend. She was preceded in death by her Grammie Jean. Karina is survived by her parents, Ron and Katie Robertson, her siblings Annika and Erik, and many adoring family members and friends.

A memorial service for Karina will be held May 8th at 3:00 p.m. at **Chapel Hill Presbyterian Church** in Gig Harbor.
A reception at the **Boys and Girls Club** is immediately following. All are welcome to come and celebrate Karina's life. She was very much loved and is greatly missed by her family and friends.

In lieu of flowers, please send donations in memory of Karina Robertson FBO Stem Cell Research to: Fred Hutchison Cancer Research Center, PO Box 19024, J5-200, Seattle, WA 98109. In addition, donations are welcome to Young Life. Please make checks to Young Life, specifying "Karina Robertson Memorial," Mail to 4020 S. 56th, Suite 210A, Tacoma, WA. 98409.

A Celebration of the Life of Karina Jean Robertson
Chapel Hill Presbyterian Church ~ May 8, 2010

Welcome and Opening Prayer
Pastor Mark Toone

"For All the Saints"

Scripture Reading - Psalm 139:1-18
Pastor Randy Rowland

Eulogy
Pastor Mark Toone

Time of Sharing
Dr. Rob Lane – Family Friend
Madeline Monson & Aundi Ragan – Friends of Karina
Sam Graham – Cousin

Video Tribute

Worship
Bill Duppenthaker

Time of Sharing
Brad Henning – Family Friend
Erin Marshall – Family Friend
Ron Robertson – Father

Scripture Reading – II Timothy 4:1-8
Wes Anderson

The Fight, the Race, the Faith
Pastor Mark Toone

Prayer of Committal
Danny DeWalt

"The Solid Rock"

Benediction
Pastor Rick Enloe

Memorial Program in Gig Harbor. More than one thousand people came to remember Karina.

KARINA ROBERTSON
LOVED BY EMERSON 2 EAST
A message shared with the girls from her college dorm at Seattle Pacific University

A friend from her college dorm and her mother
gave little fir tree seedlings to all the girls on Karina's
dorm floor. This gift struck us as very special because
of Karina's experience. A month before she died, she
woke me in the middle of the night and told
me clearly that she saw something. Karina described
it as a metaphor. I asked her what she
meant. She described a tree standing strong while other
trees were blowing in a storm. Only one tree stood
strong. As she described this, I imagined a fir tree
that meant she would stand strong during this storm
in our lives. Her tree vision encourages me to stay
strong and rooted in my faith.

The fir tree seedlings were wrapped in papers like the
one on the opposite page with the following message:

**There is a very special garden where the trees of memory
grow, nurtured by the kindness and concern that good
friends show. The roots are cherished memories of good
times in the past, the branches tender promises that souls
endure and last. It's a place of peace and beauty where
bright new hopes can start. It's memory's lovely garden
that soothes the hurting heart.**

Top photo: Roche Harbor garden, a place Karina loved and
dreamed of having her wedding.
Lower photo: Karina, Katie, and Annika in front of the
Roche Harbor garden.

Karina Robertson
Loved by Emerson 2 East

There's a very special garden
Where the trees of memory grow
Nurtured by the kindness
And concern that good friends show.
The roots are cherished memories
Of good times in the past
The branches tender promises
That souls endure and last.
It's a place of peace and beauty
Where bright new hopes can start
It's memory's lovely garden
That soothes the hurting heart.

FROM KARINA'S PRAYER JOURNAL

Lord,

　　You're in control. Sometimes I just can't understand
how You're working. I'm trying to rely on You, and You
alone, the greatest love of my life. Please show me the
direction for my life, I put it in Your hands. I know You'll
show me where to go.

Photo: The amazing rainbow that appeared at the
end of Karina's memorial service at Roche Harbor. Many
friends and family joined us to remember her at one of
Karina's favorite places.

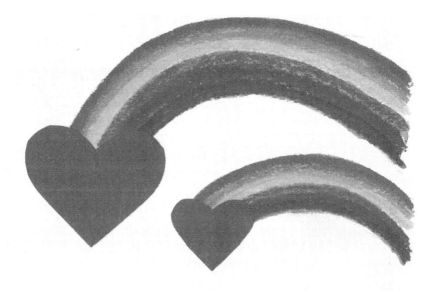

A memory of the double rainbow we got after Karina's death.
Sketch by Katie.

You're in control. Sometimes I just can't understand how You're working. I'm trying to rely on You and You alone, the greatest love of my life.

Please show me the direction for my life. I put it in Your hands. I know You'll ⬛ show ⬛ ⬛ me where to go.

189

Opposite page:

FROM KARINA'S PRAYER JOURNAL

God will lead you to the right place. He has a plan for you.

Top photo, opposite page: The rainbow that seemed to rise out of our buoy just after Karina's death. It was a comforting promise that God was with us and that we could trust him.

Lower photo opposite page: Grammie Jean (Katie's mom) and Karina, both greatly loved. Karina looked forward to seeing her grandmother in heaven.

Karina, age three, with Grammie.

you to the , God will lead
He has a plan place—
for you.

APRIL 26 DEVOTION
FROM THE DEVOTIONAL *GOD CALLING*
Our family read this devotion together on
April 26, 2010

I Make The Opportunities

Never doubt. Have no fear. Watch the faintest
tremor of fear, and stop all work, everything, and rest
before Me until you are joyful and strong again.

   Deal in the same way with all tired feelings. I was
weary too, when on earth, and I separated Myself
from My desciples and sat and rested on the well. Rested
--- and then it was that the Samaritan woman was helped.

   I had to teach renewal of Spirit --- force rest of body to My
Disciples. Then, I lay with My Head on a pillow, asleep in
the boat. It was not, as they thought, indifference. They
cried, "Master, carest thou not that we perish?" And I had
to teach them that ceaseless activity was no part of My
Father's plan.

   When Paul said, "I can do all things through Christ which
strengthenth me," he did not mean that he was to do all
things and then rely on Me to find strength. He meant that
for all I told him to do, he could rely on My supplying the
strength.

   My work in the world has been hindered by work, work,
work. Many a tireless, nervous body has driven a spirit.
The spirit should be the master always and just simply and
naturally use the body as need should arise. Rest in Me.

   Do not seek to work for Me. Never make opportunities.
Live with Me and for Me. I do the work and I make the
opportunities.

Photo: A beautiful landmark at Malibu which is also a memorial
to Karina.

I MAKE THE OPPORTUNITIES

Never doubt. Have no fear. Watch the faintest tremor of fear, and stop all work, everything, and rest before Me until you are joyful and strong again.

Deal in the same way with all tired feelings. I was weary too, when on earth, and I separated Myself from My Disciples and sat and rested on the well. Rested—and then it was that the Samaritan woman was helped.

I had to teach renewal of Spirit—force rest of body to My Disciples. Then, as your Example, I lay with My Head on a pillow, asleep in the boat. It was not, as they thought, indifference. They cried, "Master, carest thou not that we perish?" and I had to teach them that ceaseless activity was no part of My Father's plan.

When Paul said, "I can do all things through Christ which strengtheneth me," he did not mean that he was to do all things and then rely on Me to find strength. He meant that for all I told him to do, he could rely on My supplying the strength.

My Work in the world has been hindered by work, work, work. Many a tireless, nervous body has driven a spirit. The spirit should be the master always and just simply and naturally use the body as need should arise. Rest in Me.

Do not seek to work for Me. Never make opportunities. Live with Me and for Me. I do the work and I make the opportunities.

MALIBU BENCHES

Two benches were given in loving memory of Karina.
They sit looking out at the beautiful Princes Louisa Inlet.
The plaque on the back reads:

In loving memory of
Karina Jean Robertson
I can do all things through Christ who gives me strength
Philippians 4:13

September 6, 1990 - April 26, 2010

These benches provide a place for conversation, pondering
life, and enjoying God's creation.

In loving memory of

Karina Jean Robertson

*"I can do all things through Christ
who gives me strength."*
Philippians 4:13

September 6, 1990 – April 26, 2010

Chapter 17: Anchored and Rooted in Faith

Probably four weeks prior to Karina's death when we were on the critical care floor, I spent my nights next to her bed sleeping on a little cot. We were like soldiers together in the trenches fighting what was beginning to feel like a losing battle.

One night Karina awoke abruptly, waking me with urgency in her voice. "Mom", she said, "I see something. I think it's a metaphor."

Drowsy and skeptical I replied, "Really? A metaphor? At 2 in the morning?"

"Well, I see a tree," she explained, "It's standing tall and strong. All around it there's a storm and the other trees are whipping in the wind, but this one is standing strong."

As I listened intently, I envisioned a big fir tree standing tall amid a forest of other wispy trees blowing around and becoming uprooted. *There must be a meaning to this,* I thought. I had come to believe that God often gives dreams and visions to alert us as to what lies ahead. Given that Karina had been so sick yet seemed so coherent in retelling this vision, I wanted to take it seriously. I reasoned the tree that was standing firm must signify her in her fight against cancer. Surely she was going to come out of this storm standing strong. The winds of cancer would try to uproot her, but she would survive and not be felled, or so I thought.

Of course as the end drew closer and we finally lost her, I realized the metaphor was not about Karina living, but rather about staying anchored in faith amid the storms. The tree in her vision really stands for rooted faith. Cancer was her storm, but it did not uproot her faith. Instead, that faith carried her into the arms of her Savior, Jesus. My storm has been losing my beloved daughter. The storm of loss is like the strongest of winds. It can potentially devastate those who are left behind, but I too, am determined to stay anchored in the certainty of God's love and plan for me. When I run along my neighborhood route, I see a tree that stands out to me amid the others. It is fresh and green and always reminds me of Karina's words. If a tree has healthy roots, it will stand amid the storms. It is only by standing firm on the hope of Christ that I can endure and press on. I felt she somehow knew this and was giving me encouragement for life even as she lay dying. Colossians 2:6 came to mind as I reflected on her vision: "So then, just as you received Christ Jesus as Lord, continue to live in him, rooted and built up in him, strengthened in the faith…, and overflowing with thankfulness."

Just prior to the memorial, Ron and I took the girls from Karina's floor at Seattle Pacific out on *Epiphany*. We wanted to spend a little time with those who had touched Karina's life in the brief months she knew them at college. They had loved her and visited her in the hospital, and now, we all shared a common grief. It was so special to be out on the boat with these amazing young women. One of the girl's moms had been thinking about something meaningful she could give to everyone as a remembrance of Karina. She was also a woman of deep faith and had actually been praying about an appropriate gift. Without any prior knowledge of Karina's final vision, she provided little fir seedlings, one for each girl and for me as well. I was shocked, and as I told the girls of the tree metaphor Karina had, we became teary eyed. It was so touching. We were the trees left behind to weather the storm of loss, and now these little seedlings would remind us to stay rooted in hope and faith.

Ever since Karina died, I spend a lot of time thinking about what it takes to get through the devastating losses of life. The tree metaphor Karina described certainly left a real and lasting impression. But I also think about an anchor. The scripture from Hebrews 6:19 that describes hope as being like an anchor for one's soul especially speaks to me. I know from owning *Epiphany* how important is the anchor. It is not just a deck accessory. A boat's anchor, though small in size compared to that of the vessel, is heavy enough to hold firm in the midst of a strong squall, or storm. It is designed to grip into the bottom of the seabed so that even the strongest wind or current will not displace the boat or drive it onto the rocks. I find the comparison of hope to an anchor to be vivid and profound.

Last spring I was involved in organizing and launching a women's fellowship group in Gig Harbor. We named it "The Anchor" and planned to meet monthly for worship and encouragement in our faith and friendship. I was planning the first talk and had been pondering how to explain to the

197

women the anchoring points of my life and my faith. One morning while running, head down in serious focus, I asked the Lord to give me some kind of confirmation, in the form of an anchor, for me to use. When I looked up, right smack in front of me, was a sight so odd, yet amazing, it nearly took my breath away. It was a huge fir tree with a massive anchor draped around it. It was so ironic given Karina's metaphor of the tree, especially a fir tree, to now see this sight. I have no idea how the anchor could have been put there given its size and weight. I have run this path countless times, so to finally notice what has surely been right in front of me all along was stunning. This anchor sighting served as confirmation of the verse which had grounded me over the years and especially through the recent ordeal with Karina:

"We have this hope [Jesus] as an anchor for the soul, firm and secure." (Hebrews 6:19)

The shape of an anchor with the image of a cross running through the middle, perfectly illustrates the five anchor points of my life:

1. God hears you (I Peter 5:7)
2. He loves you (John 3:16)
3. He will never leave you (Matthew 28:20)
4. He will never forget you (Isaiah 49:15)
5. He always holds you (Isaiah 41:10)

These promises had held me secure throughout the various storms of my life. Now, having encountered the most heart wrenching loss a person can experience, they had really been put to the test. I sought to share with the women at the group these tried and true characteristics of God. I deeply desired for others to know He can be trusted. We can be confident in claiming them for ourselves and teaching them to our children. These points are not just for me, but for anyone who desires to anchor their life upon the solid rock of Christ.

Coming upon this anchor just as I was deep in prayer was yet another significant "God moment" for me. I felt He was giving me this amazing visual experience as a way of showing me once again, He is real. He cares about what I have been through and was leading me into opportunities where I could share His truth with others.

Over a lifetime these many providential moments add up to nothing less than sprinklings of the divine. I cannot discount them as mere coincidence. God's hand had been evident in every simple blessing to arise from our time in the valley of the shadow of death with Karina. Everywhere I turned I saw His love and care: from the first meeting with Dr. Thomas, the pediatric oncologist who "just happened to be our neighbor;" to our daughters' perfect bone marrow match; from the purchase of *Epiphany* the winter prior to Karina's illness; to the dock built up in a day on Hunt's Point; from the three perfect years after the transplant; to the random rainbow sightings that bring me comfort and joy even today. Everywhere I look the hand of God was and is orchestrating events to show His love and care.

As Karina's mom, I was her life-giver, the one who carried her tiny growing body inside mine for nine months, witnessed her entrance into the world, and nurtured her through 19 years worth of daily moments. My love for this child flowed through every vein of my body, so full at times I felt I could burst. Now, I had also been through the worst nightmare a parent can face.

I ponder another mother in history standing and watching her treasured child die. I now have a sense of how it must have felt to be Mary, standing at the foot of the cross, looking up at one most dearly loved. To realize you will never again, in this life, touch that cherished face or brush away a wisp of hair from your child's brow is a grief so immense it is unbearable. But in those moments when I am overcome with so much sadness I can hardly breathe, I imagine those penetrating eyes, full of love, and I hear Him say to me what He said to His own mother, *"It's all right."*

Sometime during the autumn season of 2011, I heard the song by Brandon Heath entitled "It's Alright." The words immediately pierced deeply into my grieving soul, giving me comfort. Brandon perfectly captured the pain I was in and the ensuing promise from Jesus that *"It's all right."* Just as Jesus comforted his mother with the words "don't cry for me, you know where I'll be," I hear Karina say the same to us.

It's Alright
Song lyrics by Brandon Heath

Tiny boat on an angry sea sails torn and tattered
How could Jesus be fast asleep, like it doesn't matter?
Soon as He opens His eyes, the storm just dies

It's alright, everything will be okay
Just hold tight, I'll be with you the whole way
When you're weak, I'll be strong
Keep going we're almost home
It's alright, everything will be okay

Mother Mary's got a broken heart, from the word's they're saying
Her baby boy's being torn apart, by the world He's saving
He says "Mother don't cry for me. You know where I will be"

No promise of an easy road, just a destination
Next time you forget your home, somebody is waiting
Soon as you open your eyes you realize

It's alright, everything will be okay
Just hold tight, I'll be with you the whole way
When you're weak, I'll be strong
Keep going we're almost home
It's alright, everything will be okay

Jesus speaks these words to everyone: it's alright. It's alright because through His death, He conquered sin once and for all. The grave could not hold him, nor can it hold us. Because of his resurrection, he has broken the grip of death, and in its place we have been given the anchor of hope. Karina is alive, and because of our faith in Jesus, we share the final destination; our ultimate home, heaven.

"For God so loved the world that He gave His one and only Son, that whoever believes in Him shall not perish but have eternal life."

John 3:16

"Karina's sunset" on the day of her memorial service.

A PICTURE MADE BY KARINA FOR HER PARENTS
In fourth grade

Finding this picture after Karina died gave me great hope
and joy.

> **I look forward
> to being welcomed by Karina
> when we arrive
> at our destination ---
> heaven, our ultimate home.**

Photo, opposite page: our family in 2009, at the Fred
Hutchinson Cancer Research Center Chef's and Wine Tasting
Dinner, where Ron spoke and Karina got to announce the total
amount raised.

IN HIS HANDS
A poem written by Katie Christmas 2011
After losing Karina

Little baby in your manger you lay
Peacefully sleeping, awaiting the new day.
Your life is ahead of you
As you await plans to unfold
Confident, resting in hands that hold.
They will carry you where they want you to go;
Always keep trusting and His unfailing love will show.
You came to shine bright
With your Father's love to share
To all of those under your care.
So in the Father's hands you lay
We know for sure we will be together someday.

Katie says, "I was struck by the significance of
Mary not knowing when Jesus was born what
was ahead of her and her son. None of us know
as mothers what will be for our children. Our children
are our greatest gift, and ultimately rest in God's hands."

Photo: Karina in her bassinet, with her favorite
blanket.

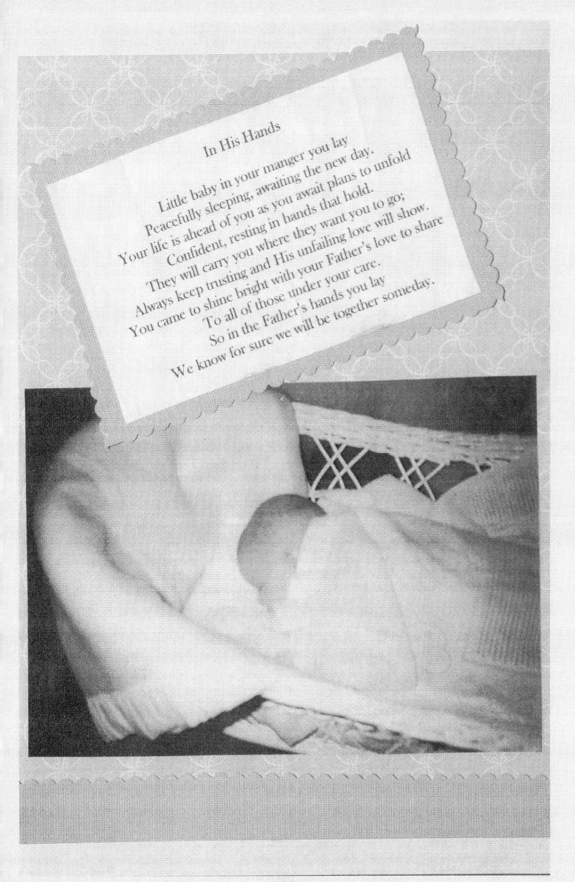

In His Hands

Little baby in your manger you lay
Peacefully sleeping, awaiting the new day.
Your life is ahead of you as you await plans to unfold
Confident, resting in hands that hold.
They will carry you where they want you to go;
Always keep trusting and His unfailing love will show.
You came to shine bright with your Father's love to share
To all of those under your care.
So in the Father's hands you lay
We know for sure we will be together someday.

Epilogue

In September of 2010, only six months after Karina's death, Ron and I
volunteered to be the summer staff coordinators at Malibu for the following 2011
season. We wanted to do something as a family to honor Karina's memory and were
therefore, very honored, when we were later chosen for the assignment. However,
we were still struggling greatly with the loss of Karina, and Ron, especially, was
reluctant to accept. Annika encouraged him. She had found solace in service to
others and explained how mentoring a group of girls and taking them to a water
skiing camp on the Columbia River had helped her move beyond her own misery.
Her words impressed him deeply. At the same time I was inspired by a book I had
been reading by Amy Carmichael. Amy experienced loss on a regular basis, as the
little Indian girls in her care, often died very young. The only way she could move
on was to keep serving those who were alive and still needed her. In the end, we
decided to go ahead with the assignment, and for one month, we lived at the camp,
directing and encouraging the college-aged volunteers. It ended up being such a
blessing for all of us, and we made enduring friendships that will last a lifetime.

Being at Malibu again brought back many memories. So much of our life had
revolved around this amazing place and all I could think about was how much I
missed Karina. Of course in my head I knew she was alright but my heart still
grasped for reassurance. I had been praying fervently for a sign to comfort me when
one day Annika walked into a room on Main Street next to the Totem Trader.
There, on the wall, was a poster-sized framed photo. Taken from behind of two
young women, in the distance, walking through what appeared to be a tunnel of
trees on the way to the outer dock. Looking closely at the photo, she knew it was
Karina. When she came and told me, I was skeptical. What was the chance a photo
of our girl would be in there? We both ran back to see, and as I studied the image it
slowly became apparent Annika was right. The height of the girl, the tiny little pony
tail on newly growing hair, the bend of the elbow, and the signature pink shorts
were unmistakable. I was completely blown away. Once again, Jesus was giving
me a sign reassuring me that everything was all right.

Prior to this, the camp manager had not known who was in the picture. He told us it had been taken during the summer of 2008. We knew that was the year Karina had attended. Later, we met the photographer who, ironically, was a family friend, Suzanne Lane. She explained she had been asked to be the camp photographer that summer and, on that particular day, had been hiding in the bushes hoping to capture a unique photo. She watched while a number of kids walked by, waiting for just the right moment. Then, just as the sun sparkled perfectly through the trees, two girls, deep in conversation walked down the boardwalk. She did not know Karina at all. She only knew it was the perfect moment for the shot. All I could do was smile at the irony of God's hand in our lives. He was reminding me, once again, Karina was not dead, just gone from my sight, on the outer dock so to speak—that is all.

"The resurrection…, is the anchor of our hope. We know that heaven is not here it's there. If we were given all we wanted here our thoughts and hearts would settle for this world rather than the next."

Elisabeth Elliot

Photo top left:

One day I was running and asking the Lord for some
kind of confirmation. I was preparing to give a talk
on being anchored in the Lord. I was praying under
my breath as I ran, wishing I could have an anchor sign,
because for me it was a symbol of rooted faith.
I looked up, and there immediately in front of me was a
huge anchor chained to a fir tree. I had run this route
hundreds of times over fifteen years, but I had never
noticed the big anchor in front of me.

Large photo: Karina is on the right wearing the pink board
shorts.

After Karina died, our family returned to Malibu in 2011
to volunteer in memory of Karina. Annika
discovered this photo on a wall on main street. The
photograph was taken in 2008, when Karina was a
camper after surviving her transplant. She was well and
happy. No one had known who the girls in the photo
were, but the camp manager had chosen to display it.
The photographer didn't know Karina at that time,
and had taken thousands of photos of the camp and
young people attending. She had positioned herself and
waited for the perfect shot, having no idea that her photo
would mean so much to us when we discovered it. It still
hangs at Malibu.

"We have
this hope
(Jesus) as
an anchor
for the
soul, firm
and
secure."
Hebrews 6:19

Top photo: Summer staff kids (college-age volunteers) at Malibu, aboard the Robertsons' boat, *Epiphany*, relaxing on a day off after serving all week at the camp.

Lower photo: the entire summer staff and coordinators.

In summer 2011, the Robertson family volunteered to work at Malibu. Ron and Katie served as Summer Staff Coordinators, and Annika and Erik were on work crew. Annika worked in the store, the Totem Trader, and Erik worked in the kitchen as dishwasher. Ron and Katie, along with friends Pat and Laura Rhoades, mentored a group of thirty seven college volunteers. As Summer Staff coordinators, Ron and Katie led Bible studies, and encouraged the staff in their faith and in their jobs. We all found serving to be a healing experience.

Our gradual healing from grief started with being thankful for the nineteen great years we had with Karina, and remembering that she is with the Lord. We have also found healing through reaching out to serve others. Serving others is what helped us most as a family. We are so thankful for our other treasures, Annika and Erik, still beside us.

Afterward
Caroline Timmins

The second time I flew out from New York for a working retreat with Katie found us in a very different season. Winter had settled over the Northwest, and the sparkling waters off their seaside home had been replaced by muddled waves of gray. A chilly mist rolled off the water, and Mt. Rainier remained hidden behind a thick curtain of fog as the sun, more stingy now, only flickered once or twice through the haze. Just as seasons change the look of nature, so loss alters the landscape of the human heart: its response varies from one person to another and from one day to the next.

By this time in the process we had settled on a name for the book. Suggested by Annika, *Anchored* seemed a perfect fit for describing Karina's life and the overall response of the family to her death. While each family member has dealt with different emotional expressions of loss, they each remain anchored on the hope of Christ.

Annika is solidly rooted in her faith, and while she misses her sister greatly, serving others has helped her deal with the grief. The summer of 2010, immediately following Karina's death, she spent a month volunteering on work crew at Malibu. She came home with a full heart, realizing that serving God through serving people and sharing her sister's life with others, was healing and rejuvenating. Annika has also made use of every opportunity to share her experience. In the fall of that same year, for her senior project at Gig Harbor High School, she organized 160 friends and family to run the Seattle half marathon in honor of Karina. Through this endeavor she raised an amazing $250,000.00 for the Fred Hutchinson Cancer Research Center (FHCRC). Another part of her project involved a "Karina Jean" sale, in which she gathered used designer jeans from the community to sell at a reduced price. These proceeds were also given to the FHCRC. This sale has now become an annual tradition.

In 2011, during the fall of her freshman year at the University of Washington, Annika was chosen by her sorority sisters to represent Alpha Chi

Omega in Delta Tau Delta's "Miss Greek" philanthropy pageant which also benefits the Fred Hutchinson Cancer Research Center. One contestant from each sorority had the task of fundraising for the FNCRC. The pageant took place on April 22, 2012, and consisted of a personality walk, talent portion, question and answer panel, and a speech on the meaning of philanthropy. Annika not only represented her sorority, but also her sister. She used the children's book she wrote and illustrated for Karina during the transplant, as her talent, and spoke in memory of Karina in her speech. Annika raised $67,000.00 for the FHCRC, a fundraising feat unprecedented in the 25 year history of the pageant. Her touching performance earned her a tiara, sash, scholarship, and the 2012 "Miss Greek" title.

Erik continues on his own private journey. His contemplative demeanor reflects the internalization of his grief but his walk of faith is quiet and steady. He has sought normalcy and routine through school and sports. Erik too, discovered an inevitable outlet for grief was serving as a family at Malibu when Ron and Katie were the summer staff coordinators. He found purpose in the simple routine of washing dishes for the camp, and also had a lot of fun. Recently he has turned to serving as a Young Life leader for freshman boys at Gig Harbor High School. Erik is a delight to everyone he encounters always evoking a laugh with his dry sense of humor.

There is no formula for dealing with grief. Katie, though generally resolved, still encounters moments of deep sadness; and Ron, after almost three years, battles other potent feelings. It would be disingenuous to pretend that facing grief with faith and hope makes dealing with the human emotions any less difficult.

One day Katie bumped into an acquaintance who inquired as to the name of the book. When she told him the one word title, the man heard it as "Angered," which Katie quickly corrected but smiled, and said, "yes, I guess it could be called that as well." She was referring to Ron's response since the death of Karina. While both believe in Jesus Christ and His promise of eternal life, they have each responded very differently emotionally. Katie has found comfort in the simple child-like faith that has been her stronghold through a variety of trials in life, while Ron has struggled greatly to make sense out of a seemingly senseless death. As mentioned earlier, when faced with circumstances in life beyond one's control, there is always a choice: submit to God and accept His greater plan, or fight and demand an answer. Neither way is wrong. Both are very normal. When tragedy strikes, anger toward God is a common human response.

213

One evening the three of us sat enjoying the fire on the partially enclosed terrace of their lovely home. The sound of the sea drifted up through the dark of night while Ron shared honestly of his feelings. He knows he is stuck in his wrath against God, and Katie agrees the rage seeps out into the rest of his life interrupting peace in the home. He willingly admits he is currently seeking counseling in hopes of finding a way out of this abyss. At times they take out their frustration on each other, and unwittingly hamper each others' freedom of expression. Such is the complex dance that often occurs in marriage following the death of a child: one spouse's emotion affects the other in a routine which can quickly disintegrate into accusations and hurt feelings. The steps must be changed if a different outcome is to be achieved.

Many issues arise both personally and relationally when a child dies, and it is very important for a couple to seek outside emotional and spiritual help if they find themselves in a locked position. Some marriages do not survive for reasons that could have been avoided if they had sought help, given each other grace amid the journey, and taken thoughtful strides toward behaving differently. Fortunately, the Robertson's are committed to sorting and cleaning out the emotional debris deposited in their lives after the storm of Karina's death. Their experience of loss has rocked their boat, but the anchor is holding firm.

Wrestling with God never weakens faith. He is merciful and full of compassion. He understands our need to try and figure things out. But often, despite our demands, we will not get the desired response. It can be infuriating, but His aim is not to frustrate. Rather, His ways are far above ours. We are given the freedom to question, but we must eventually make peace with letting God be God. We must settle in a place of child-like trust. Victory can only be achieved through this one thing: staying anchored - heart, mind, and soul - on the truth of Jesus Christ and His promise of life eternal. Karina faced down cancer and death, and remained firm in her faith till the end. Now the task for those left behind is the same: to walk by faith, anchored in hope.

"[May] Christ dwell in your hearts through faith...that you, being rooted and established in love, may have power...to grasp how wide and long and high and deep is the love of Christ, and to know this love that surpasses knowledge...Now to Him who is able to do immeasurably more than all we ask or imagine, according to His power...to Him be the glory!"

Ephesians 3:17-21

Top photo: Annika and her friends walking the
Seattle half-marathon in memory of Karina. For her
senior project, Annika organized a group of 160 people
to run and walk the race as a fundraiser to benefit
Fred Hutchinson Cancer Research Center. We called
ourselves "Team Karina Jean." Annika's project raised
$250,000 toward cancer research.

Lower photo: Erik, Annika, Katie, and Ron after the
half-marathon. We were happy to complete the thirteen
miles.

On the back of the team Karina Jean T-shirts was the verse:

2 Timothy 4:7
I have fought the good fight, I have finished the race,
I have kept the faith.

Shoe art by Katie.

Karina's sister, Annika, raised more than $65,000 for the Fred Hutchinson Cancer Research Center.

She was chosen Miss Greek 2012 at the University of Washington in a competition which included a personality walk, a question and answer panel, a speech on the meaning of philanthropy, and a talent portion. For her talent, she read her illustrated children's book, *My Sister and Me*.

My Sister and Me is available on amazon.com/books.

miss**greek** 2012

Congratulations to Annika Robertson of Alpha Chi Omega, who was crowned Miss Greek 2012 at the 26th Annual Miss Greek Pageant on Sunday, April 22, 2012.

Thanks to all of the Miss Greek contestants and the men of Delta Tau Delta who raised $65,000 for cancer research at Fred Hutchinson Cancer Research Center. With their support, and that of all contestants over the past 26 years, the Mis[...] than $1.5 million.

In loving memory of
Karina Jean Robertson
9.6.90-4.26.10

Cory Evans

For Karina

Written by family friend, Rob Lane, MD, and read at
Karina's Memorial Service
May 10, 2010

Yesterday I drove up to Mt. Rainier, to Paradise, to do some climbing and skiing. As I climbed up through the forests and glaciers of the spectacular place, I did a lot of thinking about Karina in Paradise. I wondered what she was doing right now. I know God gave us an imagination for a reason and He has given us some hints about what heaven is like. So I started imagining what Karina is doing and they were pretty fun thoughts. But rather than tell you where my imagination took me, I would encourage you to use your own. I am certain whatever she is doing, it is with Jesus and it is good, and purposeful, meaningful and a whole lot of fun. I thought back also to the hours we spent while Karina lingered in heaven's waiting room. Dr. Thomas told us a story about a young woman who had died from her leukemia some years ago and how her six year old sister had looked into her coffin and then turned to her mother and asked:

"When will the Prince come and kiss her awake?"

It did not take us long to imagine the Prince of Peace waiting to wake Karina up to new life in heaven. And when we thought that, it became harder to hold her back from Heaven's Gate.

At one time or another we will all have an opportunity to give back to the Lord someone that He has entrusted to us for a time. It may be a child, a parent, a spouse, a sibling, or a friend. And it may not really seem like a choice at all, but it is. Because when we make that choice to surrender back to God our loved ones, we acknowledge that their life was a gift on loan to us. And we acknowledge that Jesus' promises for them in heaven are true and are a source of great joy and expectation. And we acknowledge that He has a plan for us as well--not to leave that vacuum in our lives created by departure of the one we love so much, but to fill it, in His time, in ways beyond our imagining.

Right now I imagine Jesus is walking through the Garden explaining wonder upon wonder to Karina and at the same time He is planning what He will do with the lives of the Robertsons and Karl--special things that they can do only because He has prepared them by letting them know and love Karina.

A few of my amazing patients, pastors and friends have taught me that God's peace in times like this rests on a hope in Christ which is not only deep but wide. It is not only a hope of what He can and might do for us today, but if that proves to be a disappointment, we have a hope in His plans for us tomorrow, and when our tomorrows end, He has a plan for in eternity. It seems to me that when our hope for today gets out of balance with our hope for tomorrow and for eternity that peace goes away. But when we cultivate hope in all three areas, God is able to finish the good work He has started in each of us, in His time, if we let Him.

Sometimes we see something special going on in the one who is departing. Sometimes we see something special going on in the family and friends. And every now and then we see something special going on in all of them. In my years of caring for folks, we did not see that happen often, but when it did, it was always God at work. It happened here and it is happening now. Ultimately this story is not about how amazing Karina was, and still is, or about how amazing the Robertsons were, and still are, nor about how amazing their community of friends were and still are. It is about how amazing God is in all of them. And the good news is that He is waiting for each of us to figure that out so that when we have our Karina moment-- and we will, God will get to have His God moment and welcome us home. Mothers and fathers do not get to have a homecoming celebration unless the kids come home, neither does God.

Not everyone gets to go to heaven, but if you knew Karina, I am sure she is hoping that you will come and visit her some day and I am sure she wants us to know that there is only one way there. They call Him the Way and His name is Jesus.

The Hebrew people have a wonderful encouragement for each other which is perfect for us today: **REMEMBER.**
Remember what God did in Karina's life.
Remember what God is doing in the Robertsons' lives.

Remember what God is doing in our community.

And when we remember how amazing God's gift to us was in Karina, it is easier to imagine how amazing the rest of His plans for us must be--and that is something in Oswald Chamber's words, we can look forward to with "Breathless Expectation."

A PAPER KARINA WROTE IN FIFTH GRADE AT LIGHTHOUSE CHRISTIAN SCHOOL

PEACE

Peace is like soaring in the clear blue sky, Flying through the universe, Watching people working together in harmony, Seeing the quietness of the sea on a summer's day, Looking at big fluffy clouds on a gorgeous day.

Photo: Karina (visible) and Annika on the front of our boat in Princess Louisa Inlet. Summer 2009.

PEACE

Karine #1
Creativew,

Peace is like soaring in the clear blue sky, Flying through the universe, Wathing people working together in harmony, Seeing the quietness of the sea on a summer's day, Looking at big fluffy clouds on a gorgous day.

Peace I Leave with You

225

Anchor art by Katie.

Ideas for anchoring your children in faith

1. It's never too early to start talking to kids about the Lord, helping them to know how loved they are, and what a special plan God has for their lives. (Jeremiah 29: 11-13)
2. It's never too early to start helping kids memorize scripture. From age two and up kids easily repeat short phrases and songs. This scripture once hid in their hearts, will stay with them their whole lives. (Psalm 119: 11)
3. Teach your kids the simplicity of prayer: that they can come to the Lord with all of their cares and concerns, and also with gratefulness for the many blessings of life. (I Peter 5:7)
4. Teach kids to combat fear with what is true…you can nip anxiety in the bud by teaching kids to hold firmly to truth rather than the imagined "monster under the bed." (Philippians 4: 8-9)
5. Teach them the importance of time with the Lord. Kids love the idea of finding their own special, secret place where they can meet for quiet time with Him. Give your kids a children's Bible and a journal and teach them to write their thoughts and prayers in it. Help them to cultivate a personal relationship with God. As they get older this can be a habit that keeps them anchored. (Matthew 6:6)
6. Focus on the faithfulness of God in your own life and share stories about answered prayers, "God moments", and stories from the Bible or things you read about others, of His faithfulness. (Lamentations 3:23)
7. Make the most of every opportunity to show kids how God is in the details of life, and impress upon them how deeply He desires to be in relationship with us. Don't be shy about helping kids invite Christ into their heart. (Deuteronomy 6:6-9)
8. Take time for daily devotional readings together, talking about the Lord openly and showing how He is real. (Proverbs 22:6)
9. Point out the wonders of creation and the amazing patterns and things in nature that point to designs of a Master builder and Creator. (Psalms 19:1-2)

10. Make learning about God fun with songs, plays, puppet shows, and movies. (Colossians 3:23)

11. Be intentional about giving kids a wide exposure to faith activities through involvement like church, summer camps, special speakers, and concerts. (Hebrews 10:23-24)

12. Treat your family like a team: get your kids to support each other like they would team mates. Eat together. Make time for shared activities, vacations, play and conversation. (Ephesians 4:2-3)

ANCHOR POINTS

1. He Hears You!
1 Peter 5:7
Cast all you anxiety on Him,
because he cares for you.

2. He Loves You!
John 3:16
For God so loved the
world that He gave His
one and only son, that
whoever believes in him
shall not perish but have
eternal life.

3. He Never Leaves You!
Matthew 28:20
...And surely I am with you
always, to the very end of
the age.

4. He Never Forgets You!
Isaiah 49:15
Can a mother forget the
baby *in her arms* and have
no compassion on the child
she has borne? Though she
may forget, I will not forget you!

5. He Always Holds You!
Isaiah 41:10
So do not fear, for I am with
you; do not be dismayed, for
I am your God. I will
strengthen you and help
you; I will uphod you with
my righteous right hand.

Katie enjoys sharing the anchor points of faith,
incuding to schools. She also speaks on anchoring children
in faith as parents. For speaking engagements,
contact: katiejr@comcast.net
Anchor-cross (above) drawn by Annika.

Simple gifts for helping those who grieve

Being on the outside watching a friend or family member deal with grief can feel like an extremely helpless position. Following are a few "gifts" a person can offer to assist grieving loved ones in their journey through the dark night of loss.

1. **The gift of time** - grieving can be a long process, allow your friend or family member the freedom to not feel or behave "like themselves" for a good period of time. Most counselors agree grief takes at least one year and can last up to three or five years. Encouraging a person to be still, to journal, and to talk out their emotions, either with a friend, or a counselor, can greatly aid the healing process.
2. **The gift of being comfortable with tears** even if they come at inconvenient times such as social gatherings, a person needs to feel embraced and not embarrassed for the spontaneous flow of tears that fall.
3. **The gift of allowing a person the right not to want to be social**
4. **The gift of allowing a person not to be "happy" or smile** much for a long time.
5. **The gift of validation** of the vast range of feelings (guilt, sadness, anger, relief,) which arise following the death of someone precious.
6. **The gift of listening** and being comfortable with whatever emotions are being expressed or whatever spiritual questions or doubts are being experienced.
7. **The gift of practical service** stepping in and helping with housecleaning and meals knowing that grieving takes up a lot of energy and the person may not be able to function well in daily living for a long time.
8. **The gift of remembering** that holidays, birthdays, anniversary dates, will be difficult for the ones left behind and therefore, especially over the first year or so, can be soothed with recognition by other people. Especially if the loss is a child, the special dates will continue to hold meaning for that family.

9. **The gift of inquiring** throughout the following months and years as to how that person is doing. Giving the person a chance to express since often, after a period of time, they feel people are tired of hearing and they should be quiet and stop processing the loss for fear of being a burden to others.

10. **The gift of honesty** when it is obvious (after a long period of time) a person is not dealing well with a loss, is taking it out on family and friends, is over-drinking or eating or behaving in unproductive ways. Speaking the truth in love is a precious gift.

11. **The gift of prayer** both with and for people to bring them comfort amid their loss.

12. **The gift of realizing** there is no formula for grief. It looks different for everyone. There is no set pattern for how a person navigates their loss.

Acknowledgments

Katie would like to thank:

First and foremost, the Lord,

My ever-loving husband, Ron, who is a daily blessing,

Annika and Erik, my treasured children, for their support and encouragement,

My mother, Jean, for teaching me to pray,

My sister Laurie, for nurturing my faith in Jesus,

My sister Nancy for encouraging Karina and me to write a book,

My twin sister, Sara, for being my best friend,

Caroline Timmins, for writing our story, and creating collages with me,

Dawn Jimenez, for help with editing,

Chris Ballasiotes for the cover layout,

Mimmi Beck for help with the internal layout,

Suzanne Lane, for her photography,

Robert Lane M.D., for his wisdom and support as we encountered multiple rounds of cancer with Karina,

The Fred Hutchinson Cancer Research Center for their life-giving research,

Brandon Heath, for the use of his song lyrics and writing the Forward,

All those people, near and far who walked our journey with us, prayed and gave support in so many ways....we can never thank you enough for your love and care.

Caroline would like to thank:

Jesus, in whom I live and breathe and have my being,

Jeff, for his great encouragement and love,

Kaelyn and Chet, for being supportive, all-around great kids,

Katie, for entrusting me with your story,

The many Seattle Christian School teachers who supported and encouraged my passion for writing; from Mrs. Faulk, my second grade teacher, who first praised my ability, to Miss Haugen and Miss Waddell, my high school English teachers, who not only taught creative writing but also encouraged me to surrender my talents to the Lord. The foundational skills these dedicated teachers taught, and the confidence they instilled, have been enduring, precious gifts.

To the many friends and family who love and encourage me.

Thank you to Annika for drawing the anchor-cross logo which appears throughout the book.

End Notes

Chambers, O. (1986). *Devotions for a deeper life*. Cincinnati, Ohio: God's Bible School

Elliot, E. (1987). *A Chance to Die: the life and legacy of Amy Carmichael*. Revel Books.

Elliot, E. (1990). *A Path through Suffering: discovering the relationship between God's mercy and our pain*. Ventura, CA: Regal Books

Heath, Brandon; Logan, Michael; Cockrell, Thad; *It's Alright*. Lyrics from album Leaving Eden, Reunion Records, (2011)

Hurnard, H. (1975). *Hinds Feet on High Places*. Illinois: Tyndale House Publishers, Inc.

Hurnard, H., Layton, D. (1998). *Hinds Feet on High Places* (children's edition). Destiny Image Publishers

Lewis, C.S. (1956). *The Last Battle*. New York: Macmillan

Mears, H. (1990). *Dream Big*. Ventura, CA: Regal Books

Rayburn III, J. (1999). *Dance Children Dance*. Morningstar Press

Robertson, A. (2013). *My Sister and Me*. Gig Harbor: Create Space (Amazon)

Russell, A. editor at large. (1989). *God Calling*. Ohio: Barbour Publishing Inc.

Van Dyke, H. (1911). *The Poems of Henry Van Dyke*. New York: Charles Scribner and Sons

Sketch by Katie.

The "Robertson" flag by Annika.

Sketch by Annika.

Roche Harbor by Erik.

Gig Harbor Yatch Club flag.

Epiphany by Karina.

If this book has touched you, **PLEASE WRITE US A REVIEW on www.amazon.com/books to help our book reach other readers**. You need not have purchased the book on amazon.com to write a review. To leave your comments, simply go to amazon.com/books, search for our title, click on it, and scroll down to "write a customer review."

To hear of up- coming events, listen to the song "It's Alright" by Brandon Heath, or learn more, check out our website: www.anchoredthebook.com

To order books, for questions and comments, or for speaking engagements, please email Katie Robertson at: katiejr@comcast.net

Made in the USA
Charleston, SC
03 May 2013